# Juz' 'Amma: 30

*(With Al-Fātiḥah)*

## For The Classroom

PART 30 OF THE HOLY QUR'ĀN

Junior Level

## Volume 2

***From Al-Balad 90 to An-Naba' 78***

**Arabic Text, Transliteration, Translations, and Explanation**

Translations

'Abdullāh Yūsuf 'Ali & Muḥammad Marmarduke Pickthal

Rendered into Modern English

*Compilation and Explanation*

*Abidullah Ghazi*

IQRA'

International Educational Foundation

# Part of a Comprehensive and Systematic Program of Islamic Studies

**A Textbook for**
**Qur'anic Studies**
**Junior Level/General**

***Juz' 'Amma: 30, Vol. 2***

**Chief Program Editors**
Dr. Abidullah al-Ansari Ghazi
(Ph.D. History of Religion, Harvard University)

Dr. Tasneema Ghazi
(Ph.D. Curriculum-Reading, University of Minnesota)

**Reviewed by**
Fadel Abdallah
(M.A. Arabic Islamic Studies, University of Minnesota)

Dr. Robert N. Delk
(Ph. D., University of Wisconsin)

Maulana Shuaib-ud-Din
(Fadil Dar ul-Ulum, Karachi)

Fouad Al-Mimouni
(M.A., English Literature)

**Language Editing**
Dr. Khwaja Moinul Hassan
(Ph. D.English, Purdue University)

Mahlaqa Patel
(Student, University of Illinois, Chicago)

Suhaib H. Ghazi
(B.A., University of Redlands)

**English Typesetting**
Ammar Ansari
(M.S., University of Illinois, Chicago)

**Arabic Typesetting**
Randa Zaiter
(B.S. Social Science, University of Lebanon)

**Cover Design**
Jennifer Mazzoni
(B.A. Illustration, Columbia College Chicago)

**Acknowledgments:**
Our thanks are due to Sheik Abdur Rahman, M.D. and his wife, Mrs. Sadiqua Rahman, of Cincinnati for their encouragement and support.



Second printing 1998
Third printing June 2000
Fourth printing April 2002
Fifth Printing September 2006
Sixth Printing January 2009
Seventh Printing June 2012
Eighth Printing March 2015
**Printed in India**



Library of Congress Catalog Card Number: 95-77845
ISBN 1-56316-110-9

بِسۡمِ ٱللَّهِ ٱلرَّحۡمَٰنِ ٱلرَّحِيمِ

إِنَّمَا نُطۡعِمُكُمۡ لِوَجۡهِ ٱللَّهِ لَا نُرِيدُ مِنكُمۡ
جَزَآءً وَلَا شُكُورًا ﴿٩﴾

*We feed you only for the countenance of Allah. We wish not from you reward or gratitude.*

(The Holy Qur’an, 76:9)

مَا نَقَصَ مَالٌ مِن صَدَقَة

IQRA’ wishes to thank Zakat Foundation for their contribution to the printing of this book. Please visit the Zakat Foundation of America at **www.zakat.org** to support their many noble and much needed causes.

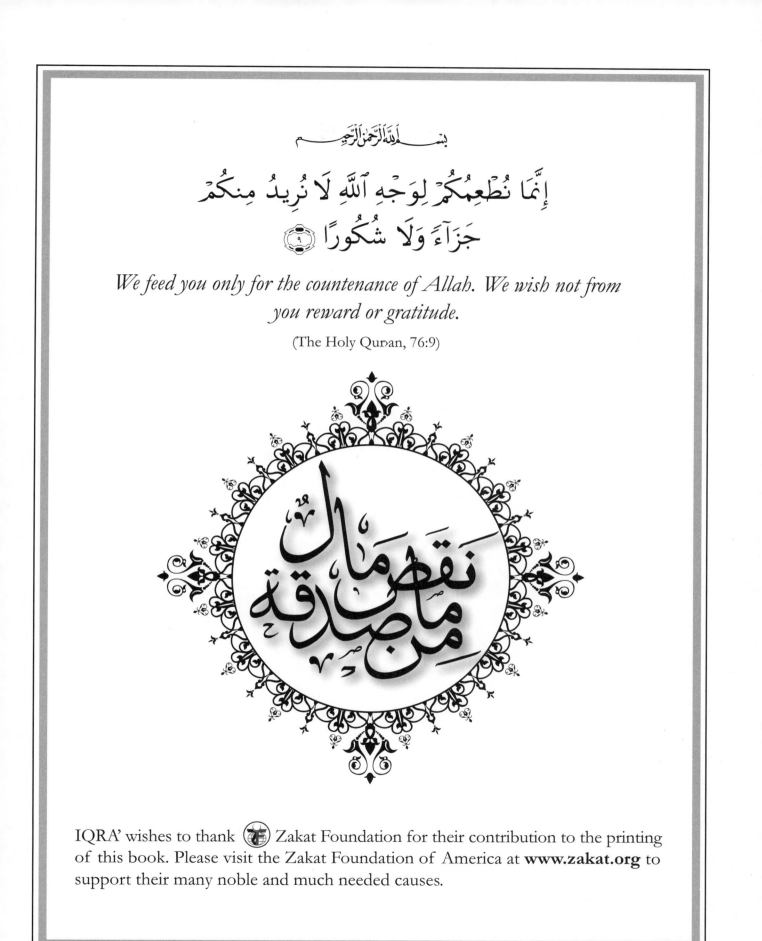

# Table of Contents

بِسْمِ اللّٰهِ الرَّحْمٰنِ الرَّحِيْمِ

# JUZ' 'AMMA: 30

## IQRA'S NOTE: TO PARENTS AND TEACHERS

IQRA' International is pleased to offer two textbooks at the junior level: ***Juz' 'Amma: 30, Volume 1 (From An-Nās:114 to Ash-Shams: 89 with Sūrah Al-Fātiḥah, 1) and Juz' 'Amma:30, Volume 2 (From Al-Balad:90 to An-Naba':78).*** The order of the *Suwar,* in these textbooks, is reversed to facilitate the reading , memorization and understanding of the shorter *Suwar* before the longer *Suwar.*

Most of the *Suwar* in the last *Juz'* (30) are Makkan and deal with the theme of *Tawḥīd* (The Oneness of Allāh), *The Risālah* (Prophethood), *Al-'Ākhirah,* (the Hereafter), establishment of the *Qiyāmah,* (The Day of Judgment), the pleasure of *Jannah* and the ordeals of *Jahannam.* These enjoin virtues such as faith, patience, perseverance, trust, hope, generosity and honesty. These encourage social justice, care for the relatives, poor and needy, concern for neighbors, fair dealings, respect for life, freedom of worship, religious tolerance and hospitality. These condemn disbelief, debauchery, falsehood, scandals, miserliness, oppression and arrogance. These were the teachings of the Qur'ān which, under the guidance of the Prophet ﷺ, inspired the Makkans and early converts, brought them into the fold of Islam and prepared them for the greatest sacrifices.

These two textbooks with accompanying workbooks provide, for both an interested reader and a teacher of Qur'ānic Studies, the opportunity to understand the basic teachings of the Qur'ān on some key concepts as presented, so powerfully and graphically, in the early Makkan *Suwar.*

The teachers may be aware of our earlier publications, *Short Sūrahs* and *Teachings of the Qur'ān*: *Volume 1* (now Volumes I, II, III and IV are also available), written as textbooks at elementary level which have been received with great enthusiasm in the class-rooms. These textbooks represented the first attempt to systematically introduce the Message of the Qur'ān to our children at their level of comprehension.

This textbook is a part of IQRA'*s Comprehensive and Systematic Program of Islamic Studies* which encompasses four levels: *Pre-School, Elementary.*

**Division of the Juz':** Juz' 'Amma has been divided into two volumes; the first contains twenty-six (26) *lessons* covering twenty-five (25) *Suwar* and the second volume contains twenty-four (24) *lessons* covering thirteen (13) *Suwar*. Each *Sūrah* starts with an introduction, its title in Arabic, *Sūrah* number and the number of the *'Āyāt*. Each short *Sūrah* is treated as one complete lesson, while the longer *Suwar* are divided into two or more lessons. When the long *Sūrah* is divided into two lessons the introduction is not repeated.

**Lesson Plan:** Each lesson contains ***Introduction, Arabic text, transliteration, translations*** ('Abdullāh Yūsuf 'Ali and M. M. Pickthal)***, explanation, We Have Learned, and a complete vocabulary of Arabic text***; each part of the lesson plan needs some further explanation.

**Transliteration:** In transliteration we follow the Library of Congress System with few modifications (See Appendix I). We have followed phonetic method to facilitate the reading. The Arabic definite article *(al)* often assimilates its initial (a) in speech while in writing it does appear. Following the phonetic scheme we have not written it in transliteration. A letter appearing in the text but falling silent after the *'Āyah* is shown in the vocabulary within parenthesis. In transliterating the *Sūrah* we have followed only phonetic sound (as it must be pronounced before the *'Āyah*). The *ḥarakāt* (*i'rāb*) do appear before or after the consonant letter of the *'Āyah* but they are not read. We have put the silent *ḥarakāt* in parenthesis. For example:

1:1. *Rabbi al-'ālamīna* is written as *Rabbi-(a)l-'ālamīn(a)* and read as *Rabbi-l-'ālamīn*
114:1. *Bi-Rabbi an-nāsi* is written as *Bi-Rabbi-(a)n-nās(i)* and read as *Bi-Rabbi-n-nās*
*Fi Al-Qur'āni al-Karīmi* is transliterated as *fi-(a)l-Qur'āni-(a)l-Karīm(i) and read as fi-l-Qur'āni-l-Karīm*

We have followed the phonetic rule in the usage of *Shamsi* (Sun) letters for example:

1:1 *Al-Raḥmāni Al-Raḥīmi* is transliterated as *Ar-Raḥmāni-(a)r-Raḥīm(i)* and read as *Ar-Raḥmāni-r-Raḥīm*
114:1 *'Ilāhi al-nāsi* is transliterated as *'Ilāhi-(a)n-nās(i)* and read as *Ilāhi-n-nās* .

The *Sūrah* is written in Arabic and transliterated in English to help facilitate the reader's pronunciation in case he/she has not yet learned to read the Arabic script. However, it is the policy of IQRA' not to encourage this practice and the entire program of IQRA' is designed to teach the students reading and understanding of Qur'ānic Arabic. We shall soon publish another edition of this textbook without transliteration for those who want to develop Arabic reading skills without depending on transliteration.

**Translations:** We have provided two major translations of 'Abdullāh Yūsuf 'Ali (the first translation) and Muḥammad Marmaduke Pickthal (the second translation) side by side. These original translations from Old English are rendered into Modern English. A student would greatly benefit by the understanding of the Qur'ān from these two prominent scholars, he/she will also understand the difficulties of translating Arabic text. We have replaced the Old English with the Modern English without tampering with the text at all. We have also used more accepted Islamic terminology (e.g. Allāh for God, Messenger for Apostle etc.).

**Commentary:** We have used traditional authentic sources to give accepted version of the verses. We have, however, kept the comments to the minimum and allowed the text to speak for itself.

**We Have Learned:** deals with the central message of the *Sūrah* and reinforces what has been learned.

**Vocabulary:** The transliteration and the meaning of each word is provided for every *Sūrah* at the end of each lesson. The repetition of the word and careful selection of vocabulary will greatly enhance the student's understanding of the Qur'ānic text and will facilitate him/her in learning Arabic.

Workbooks based on the pattern of our completed and familiar *Sīrah Program* are under publication to provide for reinforcement, develop educational skills and provide further practice.

This work is a major effort to introduce the meaning and message of the Qur'ān at every level and we pray to Allāh سبحانه وتعالى to accept this effort and make it useful to all the lovers of the truth as contained in the Holiest Book and the Purest of the Messages.

As a concerned parent and teacher, we urge you to support this pioneering educational effort through your *Du'ā'*, advice and financial contributions. IQRA' International invites you to participate in our educational vision by:

*a) Becoming Ansars of Iqra' Educational Program,*
*b) Enrolling as members of Iqra' Book Club.*

We shall appreciate your opinion and comments to help us improve the revised edition.

Chief Editors
831 S. Laflin, Chicago, IL. 60607

Friday (*Ramaḍān* 27) February 27, 1995

سُورَةُ الْبَلَدِ

**Lesson 1**

## *AL-BALAD, 90:1-10*

### THE CITY / THE CITY

**Revealed in Makkah**

---

**INTRODUCTION:**

This *Sūrah* belongs to the early Makkan period. At the time of this Revelation, opposition toward Rasūlullāh ﷺ and his message had greatly increased. In the city of Makkah, where even the killing of an animal was not permitted, a kind and pious person such as Rasūlullāh ﷺ was opposed, tortured and oppressed. The *Sūrah* explains the two separate paths of righteousness and falsehood, and the freedom we have been given to choose between the two.

| **TRANSLITERATION:** | **ARABIC TEXT:** |
|---|---|
| *Bismillāhi-(a)r-Raḥmāni-(a)r-Raḥīm(i)* | بِسْمِ اللَّهِ الرَّحْمَٰنِ الرَّحِيمِ |
| *1. Lā 'uqsimu bi-hā<u>dh</u>a-(a)l-balad(i)* | -لَا أُقْسِمُ بِهَٰذَا الْبَلَدِ ۝ |
| *2. Wa'anta ḥillun bi-hā<u>dh</u>a-(a)l-balad(i)* | -وَأَنتَ حِلٌّ بِهَٰذَا الْبَلَدِ ۝ |
| *3. Wa wālidin wa mā walad(a)* | -وَوَالِدٍ وَمَا وَلَدَ ۝ |
| *4. Laqad <u>kh</u>alaqnā-(a)l-'insāna fī kabad(in)* | -لَقَدْ خَلَقْنَا الْإِنسَانَ فِي كَبَدٍ ۝ |
| *5. 'A-yaḥsabu 'an-lan-yaqdira 'alaihi 'aḥad(un)* | -أَيَحْسَبُ أَن لَّن يَقْدِرَ عَلَيْهِ أَحَدٌ ۝ |
| *6. Yaqūlu 'ahlaktu mālan lubadā(n)* | -يَقُولُ أَهْلَكْتُ مَالًا لُّبَدًا ۝ |
| *7. 'A-yaḥsabu 'al -lam yara-hu 'aḥad(un)* | -أَيَحْسَبُ أَن لَّمْ يَرَهُ أَحَدٌ ۝ |
| *8. 'A-lam naj'al la-hū 'ainain(i)* | -أَلَمْ نَجْعَل لَّهُ عَيْنَيْنِ ۝ |
| *9. Wa lisānan wa <u>sh</u>afatain(i)* | -وَلِسَانًا وَشَفَتَيْنِ ۝ |
| *10. Wa hadainā-hu-(a)n-najdain(i)* | -وَهَدَيْنَاهُ النَّجْدَيْنِ ۝ |

## TRANSLATIONS:

In the name of Allāh, Most Gracious, Most Merciful.

1. I do call to witness this city;
2. And you are a freeman of this city;
3. And (the mystic ties of) Parent and child;
4. Truly We have created Man into toil and struggle.
5. Does he think, that none has power over him?
6. He may say (boastfully): "Wealth have I squandered in abundance!"
7. Does he think that none sees him?
8. Have We not made for him a pair of eyes?
9. And a tongue, and a pair of lips?
10. And shown him the two highways?

In the name of Allāh, the Beneficent, the Merciful.

1. Nay, I swear by this city,
2. And you are an indweller of this city,
3. And the begetter and that which he begot,
4. We verily have created man in an atmosphere:
5. Thinks he that none has power over him?
6. And he said: I have destroyed vast wealth:
7. Thinks he that none beholds him?
8. Did We not assign to him two eyes
9. And a tongue and two lips,
10. And guide him to the parting of the mountain ways?

---

## EXPLANATION:

90:1-2. In these verses, Allāh ﷻ swears by the Holy City of Makkah, in which Rasūlullāh ﷺ resided. This city was honored through its association with the birth of Rasūlullāh ﷺ, yet at the time of this Revelation, the City was hostile to his message.

90:3. There are two explanations for the term "the begetter and that he begot," found in this verse. More specifically, it refers to Adam ﵇ and his children. It also compares the bond present between father and son with the link that this city had with its most unique son, Muhammad ﷺ. This bond may have been strained, but it could never be severed.

90:4. The struggle of mankind has two meanings here. Firstly, from the time of conception till the time of death, humans undergo great trials and tribulations. These are natural phenomena and no one can do anything to prevent them from happening. Secondly, this verse makes reference to the struggles human beings undergo to achieve their objectives in life. No one can achieve a desired goal without exertion and labor.

90:5-7. In spite of this humble quality found in man, he is proud. He believes that he is not responsible for whatever actions he may do, good or bad, and that no one watches over him.

If he is wealthier , he squanders his wealth to please himself and to achieve his objectives. He knows that his money will buy him political power, social respect and influence in society, yet, he does not realize that all such gains are merely temporary.

The rich *Kuffār* spent their resources in trying to prevent the spread of Islam, believing that their actions would succeed in stopping the Islamic message.

90:8-10. In their pride, human beings often forget that Allāh ﷻ has given them life, which takes the outer form of a beautiful body and the inner form of a soul. Through the eyes he has been given, he can see clearly. Through the tongue and lips he has been given, he can eat to sustain himself, and speak to express himself.

Here, two faculties, sight and speech, are specifically mentioned because *'Āayah* 10 refers to the two ways of Righteousness and Evil. Man especially needs these two faculties to enable him to make sound decisions for himself, and for inviting others to follow him in doing good.

**<u>WE HAVE LEARNED</u>:**

* All human beings have to struggle to achieve their desired goals in life.
* Both our faculties and our wealth is a trust of Allāh ﷻ .
* We are accountable for this trust both in this world and in the Hereafter.

**VOCABULARY**

**٩٠- سُورَةُ ٱلْبَلَدِ**

| | | |
|---|---|---|
| ١-لَا أُقْسِمُ | *Lā-'uqsimu* | Nay, I call to witness, I swear |
| بِهٰذَا الْبَلَدِ | *bi-hādha-(a)l-balad(i)* | by this city |
| ٢-وَأَنْتَ حِلٌّ | *Wa-'anta ḥill(un)* | And you are a free man, you are a dweller |
| بِهٰذَا ٱلْبَلَدِ | *Bi-hādha-(a)l-balad(i)* | of this city |
| ٣-وَوَالِدٍ | *Wa-wālid(in)* | By the father, the begetter |
| وَمَا وَلَدَ | *wa-ma walad(a)* | and the son that which he begets |
| ٤-لَقَدْ خَلَقْنَا | *laqad khalaq-nā* | Truly, We have created |

| | | |
|---|---|---|
| اَلْاِنْسَانَ | *'al-'insāna* | the man, humankind |
| فِى كَبَدٍ | *fī kabad(in)* | in toil, in an atmosphere of struggle |
| ٥-أَيَحْسَبُ أَنْ | *'A-yaḥsabu 'an* | Does he think that |
| لَنْ يَقْدِرَ | *lan yaqdira* | none has power |
| عَلَيْهِ أَحَدٌ | *'alaihi 'aḥad(un)* | over him no one |
| ٦-يَقُولُ | *Yaqūlu* | He says, he claims |
| أَهْلَكْتُ مَالاً | *'ahlaktu māla(n)* | I have spent wealth |
| لُبَداً | *lubadā(n)* | abundant |
| ٧-أَيَحْسَبُ أَنْ | *'A-yaḥsabu 'an* | Does he think that |
| لَمْ يَرَهُ أَحَدٌ | *lam yara-hū 'aḥad(un)* | no one sees him |
| ٨-أَلَمْ نَجْعَل لَّهُ | *'A-lam naj'al la-hū* | Have We not made to him |
| عَيْنَيْنِ | *'ainain(i)* | two eyes |
| ٩-وَلِسَانًا | *Wa-lisānan* | And a tongue |
| وَشَفَتَيْنِ | *wa-<u>sh</u>afatain(i)* | And two lips |
| ١٠-وَهَدَيْنَٰهُ | *Wa-hadainā-hu* | And shown him, guided him |
| اَلنَّجْدَيْنِ | *'an-najdain(i)* | the two highways, the two mountain ways |

*Lesson 2*

# *AL-BALAD, 90:11-20*

## THE CITY / THE CITY

**Revealed in Makkah**

---

| TRANSLITERATION: | ARABIC TEXT: |
|---|---|
| 11. *Fa-la-(a)qtaḥama-(a)l- ‘aqabah(ta)* | -فَلَا ٱقْتَحَمَ ٱلْعَقَبَةَ ○ |
| 12. *Wa mā ’adrā-ka ma-(a)l-‘aqabah(tu)* | -وَمَآ أَدْرَىٰكَ مَا ٱلْعَقَبَةُ ○ |
| 13. *Fakku raqabah(tin)* | -فَكُّ رَقَبَةٍ ○ |
| 14. *’Aw ’iṭ‘āmun fī yawmin dhī masghabah(tin)* | -أَوْ إِطْعَٰمٌ فِى يَوْمٍ ذِى مَسْغَبَةٍ ○ |
| 15. *Yatīman dhā maqrabah(tin)* | -يَتِيمًا ذَا مَقْرَبَةٍ ○ |
| 16. *’Aw miskīnan dhā matrabah(tin)* | -أَوْ مِسْكِينًا ذَا مَتْرَبَةٍ ○ |
| 17. *Thumma kāna mina-(a)lladhīna ’āmanū* | -ثُمَّ كَانَ مِنَ ٱلَّذِينَ ءَامَنُوا۟ |
| *wa tawāṣaw bi-(a)ṣ-ṣabri wa tawāṣaw bi-(a)l-marḥamah(ti)* | وَتَوَاصَوْا۟ بِٱلصَّبْرِ وَتَوَاصَوْا۟ بِٱلْمَرْحَمَةِ ○ |
| 18. *’Ulā’ika ’aṣḥābu-(a)l-maimanah(ti)* | -أُو۟لَٰٓئِكَ أَصْحَٰبُ ٱلْمَيْمَنَةِ ○ |
| 19. *Wa-(a)lladhīna kafarū bi’āyāti-nā* | -وَٱلَّذِينَ كَفَرُوا۟ بِـَٔايَٰتِنَا |
| *hum ’aṣḥābu-(a)l-mash’amah(ti)* | هُمْ أَصْحَٰبُ ٱلْمَشْـَٔمَةِ ○ |
| 20. *‘Alai-him nārun mu’ṣadah(tun)* | -عَلَيْهِمْ نَارٌ مُّؤْصَدَةٌۢ ○ |

**TRANSLATIONS:**

11. But he has made no haste on the path that is steep.

11. But he has not attempted the Ascent,

12. And what will explain to you
the path that is steep?
13. (It is:) freeing the bondman;
14. Or the giving of food in a day of privation
15. To the orphan with claims of relationship,
16. Or to the indigent (down) in the dust.
17. Then will he be of those who believe,
and enjoin patience,
(constancy, and self restraint),
and enjoin Deeds of kindness and compassion.
18. Such are the Companions of the
Right Hand.
19. But those who reject our Signs, they are
the (unhappy) Companions of the Left Hand.
20. On them will be Fire vaulted
over (all round).

12. Ah, what will convey to you
what the Ascent is?
13 (It is) to free a slave,
14 And to feed in the day of hunger
15. An orphan near of kin,
16. Or some poor wretch in misery,
17. And to be of those who believe
and exhort one another to
perseverance
and exhort one another to pity.
18. Their place will be on the
right hand.
19. But those who disbelieve Our revelations, their place will be on the left hand.
20. Fire will be an awning
over them.

---

**EXPLANATION**:

90:11-18. The path of Righteousness is not always easy to follow. It is an uphill struggle (v.11-12). It is a path of charity, generosity, kindness and patience.

Four things are described as the way of Righteousness: two outer actions and two inner attitudes. Outer actions include granting a slave freedom (or freeing someone of his needs) and feeding and supporting an orphan or a needy person. Inner attitudes include enjoining patience and enjoining kindness. The Righteous people who possess these traits are called "the People of the Right Hand." This is a Qur'ānic description of the joyous people of *Jannah*.

90:19-20. Those who reject the Truth and do not heed Allāh's Signs are called "the Companions of the Left Hand." This is the Qur'ānic description of the people of *Jahannam* (the Fire).

**WE HAVE LEARNED**:

* All Human beings must struggle to achieve their objectives.
* To help those who are in need is part of one's faith.
* The way of Righteousness is difficult to adhere to, but it always leads to success and *Jannah*.

## VOCABULARY II

### سُورَةُ ٱلْبَلَدِ

| | | |
|---|---|---|
| ١١-فَلَا ٱقْتَحَمَ | *Fa-la-(a)qtaḥama* | But he has not attempted |
| ٱلْعَقَبَةَ | *'al-'aqabah(ta)* | the steep path, the ascent |
| ١٢-وَمَآ أَدْرَٰكَ | *Wa-mā 'adrā-ka* | And what will explain to you |
| مَا ٱلْعَقَبَةُ | *mā-(a)l-'aqabah(tu)* | What the steep path is ? What the ascent is |
| ١٣-فَكُّ | *Fakku* | It is freeing |
| رَقَبَةٍ | *raqabah(tin)* | a slave, a neck |
| ١٤-أَوْ إِطْعَٰمٌ | *'Aw 'iṭ'ām(un)* | Or feeding |
| فِى يَوْمٍ | *fi yawm(in)* | on a day |
| ذِى مَسْغَبَةٍ | *dhi masghabah(tin)* | of hunger, of privation |
| ١٥-يَتِيمًا | *Yatīm(an)* | An orphan |
| ذَا مَقْرَبَةٍ | *dhā maqrabah(tin)* | near of kin, having kinship |
| ١٦-أَوْ مِسْكِينًا | *'Aw miskīnan* | Or an indigent, or very poor |
| ذَا مَتْرَبَةٍ | *dhā matrabah(tin)* | in the dust, in miserable condition |
| ١٧-ثُمَّ كَانَ | *Thumma kāna* | Then, again be |
| مِنَ ٱلَّذِينَ | *min '(a)lladhīna* | among those, of those |
| ءَامَنُوا | *'āmanū* | who believe |
| وَتَوَاصَوْا | *wa-tawāṣaw* | and enjoin each other |
| بِٱلصَّبْرِ | *bi-(a)ṣ-ṣabri* | to the patience, |
| وَتَوَاصَوْا | *wa-tawāṣaw* | and enjoin each other |
| بِٱلْمَرْحَمَةِ | *bi-(a)l-marḥamah(ti)* | to deeds of kindness |

| | | |
|---|---|---|
| ١٨-أُولَٰٓئِكَ | *'Ulā'ika* | Those are |
| أَصْحَٰبُ ٱلْمَيْمَنَةِ | *'aṣḥabu-(a)l-maimanat(i)* | companions of the right hand |
| ١٩-وَٱلَّذِينَ | *Wa-(a)lladhīna* | But those who |
| كَفَرُوا بِأَيَٰتِنَا | *kafarū-bi-'āyāti-nā* | reject Our signs, disbelieve in Our Revelations |
| هُمْ | *hum* | they are |
| أَصْحَٰبُ ٱلْمَشْـَٔمَةِ | *'aṣḥābu-(a)l-mash'amah(ti)* | companions of the left hand |
| ٢٠-عَلَيْهِمْ | *'Alai-him* | On them |
| نَارٌ مُّؤْصَدَةٌ | *nārun mu'ṣadah(tun)* | (will be) fire vaulted all around |

سُورَةُ الْفَجْرِ — آياتها ٣٠ — ترتيبها ٨٩

*Lesson 3*

# *AL-FAJR, 89:1-16*
## THE DAWN / THE DAWN
**Revealed in Makkah**

---

**INTRODUCTION:**

This *Sūrah* is one of the first ten *Suwar* to be revealed in Makkah during the early stages of Rasūlullāh's ﷺ mission.

Through contrast of nature and by reference to the past, Allāh ﷻ demonstrates His power to destroy evil and make good ultimately triumph over it. The evils prevalent in Makkan society during that time are recounted, and a warning of the Day of Chastisement is issued. However, Allāh ﷻ says that the righteous souls will receive a pleasing reward from their Lord.

| **TRANSLITERATION:** | **ARABIC TEXT:** |
| --- | --- |
| *Bismillāhi-(a)r-Raḥmāni-(a)r-Raḥīm(i)* | بِسْمِ اللَّهِ الرَّحْمَٰنِ الرَّحِيمِ |
| 1. *Wa-(a)l-Fajr(i)* | -وَالْفَجْرِ ۝ |
| 2. *Wa layālin 'ashr(in)* | -وَلَيَالٍ عَشْرٍ ۝ |
| 3. *Wa-(a)sh-shaf'i wa-(a)l-watr(i)* | -وَالشَّفْعِ وَالْوَتْرِ ۝ |
| 4. *Wa-(a)l-laili 'idhā yasr(i)* | -وَاللَّيْلِ إِذَا يَسْرِ ۝ |
| 5. *Hal fī dhālika qasamun lidhī ḥijr(in)* | -هَلْ فِي ذَٰلِكَ قَسَمٌ لِّذِي حِجْرٍ ۝ |
| 6. *'A-lam tara kaifa fa'ala Rabbu-ka bi-'Ād(in)* | -أَلَمْ تَرَ كَيْفَ فَعَلَ رَبُّكَ بِعَادٍ ۝ |
| 7. *'Irama dhāti-(a)l-'imād(i)* | -إِرَمَ ذَاتِ الْعِمَادِ ۝ |
| 8. *'Allatī lam-yukhlaq mithlu-hā fi-(a)l-bilād(i)* | -الَّتِي لَمْ يُخْلَقْ مِثْلُهَا فِي الْبِلَادِ ۝ |
| 9. *Wa thamūd-al-ladhīna jābu-(a)ṣ-ṣakhra bi-(a)l-wād(i)* | -وَثَمُودَ الَّذِينَ جَابُوا الصَّخْرَ بِالْوَادِ ۝ |

| | |
|---|---|
| 10. *Wa Fir‘awna dhi-(a)l-’awtād(i)* | وَفِرْعَوْنَ ذِى الْأَوْتَادِ ۝ |
| 11. *’Alladhīna ṭaghaw fi-(a)l-bilād(i)* | الَّذِينَ طَغَوْا فِى الْبِلَادِ ۝ |
| 12. *Fa-’aktharū fī-ha-(a)l-fasād(a)* | فَأَكْثَرُوا فِيهَا الْفَسَادَ ۝ |
| 13. *Fa-ṣabba ‘alai-him Rabbu-ka sawṭa ‘adhāb(in)* | فَصَبَّ عَلَيْهِمْ رَبُّكَ سَوْطَ عَذَابٍ ۝ |
| 14. *’Inna Rabba-ka labi-(a)l-mirṣād(i)* | إِنَّ رَبَّكَ لَبِالْمِرْصَادِ ۝ |
| 15. *Fa-’amma-(a)l-’insānu ’idhā ma-(a)btalā-hu Rabbu-hū* | فَأَمَّا الْإِنسَانُ إِذَا مَا ابْتَلَاهُ رَبُّهُ |
| *fa-’akrama-hū wa na‘‘ama-hū fa-yaqūlu Rabbī ’akraman(i)* | فَأَكْرَمَهُ وَنَعَّمَهُ فَيَقُولُ رَبِّى أَكْرَمَنِ ۝ |
| 16. *Wa ’ammā ’idhā ma-(a)btalā-hu fa-qadara* | وَأَمَّا إِذَا مَا ابْتَلَاهُ فَقَدَرَ |
| *‘alai-hi rizqa-hū fa-yaqūlu Rabbī ’ahānan(i)* | عَلَيْهِ رِزْقَهُ فَيَقُولُ رَبِّى أَهَانَنِ ۝ |

**TRANSLATIONS:**

In the name of Allāh, Most Gracious,
Most Merciful.

1. By the Break of Day;
2. By the Nights twice five;
3. By the Even and Odd (contrasted);
4. And by the night when it passes away;
5. Is there (not) in these an adjuration (or evidence) for those who understand?
6. Do you not see how your Lord dealt with the ‘Āad (people),
7. Of the (city of) Iram, with lofty pillars,
8. The like of which were not produced in (all) the Land?
9. And with the Thamūd (people), who cut out (huge) rocks in the valley?
10. And with Pharaoh, Lord of Stakes?

In the name of Allāh, the Beneficent,
the Merciful.

1. By the Dawn
2. And ten nights,
3. And the Even and the Odd,
4. And the night when it departs,
5. There surely is an oath for the thinking man.
6. Dost you not consider how your Lord dealt with the (tribe of) ‘Āad,
7. With many-columned Iram,
8. The like of which was not created in the lands;
9. And with (the tribe of) Thamūd, who clove the rocks in the valley;
10. And with Pharaoh, firm of might,

11. (All) these transgressed beyond
bounds in the lands.
12. And heaped therein mischief (on mischief).
13. Therefore your Lord poured on them
a scourge of diverse chastisement:
14. For your Lord is
(as a Guardian) on a watch-tower.
15. Now, as for man, when his Lord tries him,
giving him honor and gifts,
then he says, (puffed up),
"My Lord has honored me,"
16. But when He tries him, restricting His
subsistence for him, then says he (in despair),
"My Lord has humiliated me!"

11. Who (all) were rebellious (to Allāh)
in these lands,
12. And multiplied iniquity therein?
13. Therefore your Lord poured on them
the disaster of His punishment.
14. Lo! your Lord is
ever watchful.
15. As for man, whenever his Lord tries him
by honoring him, and is gracious to him
he says:
My Lord honoreth me,
16. But whenever He tries by straightening
his means of life, he says:
My Lord despises me.

---

**<u>EXPLANATION</u>:**

89:1-5. In these verses, Allāh سبحانه وتعالى swears by three things: the morning, the odd and even nights of *Dhu-(a)l-Ḥijjah*, and the night. He then asks us, "Is not in these oaths, signs for the thinking person?"

Many explanations have been offered for these oaths. Firstly, these oaths demonstrate Allāh's system of creation and natural order. Secondly, they reflect upon the rhythm of life. Thirdly, the oath of odd and even encompasses all created things; either a creation is found singular in nature or it is found in pairs. All of these demonstrate Allāh's creative and regulatory powers.

89:6-12. These verses speak of the People of ʿĀd, who had built a great civilization of huge palaces with massive pillars; of <u>Th</u>amūd, who carved their homes from mountains; and of the mighty *Fir'awn* (Pharaoh) of Egypt; all of whom defied the Prophets of Allāh سبحانه وتعالى, and created mischief in the land.

89:13-14. For their defiance, Allāh's punishment had been swift and severe. He permits the proud to be disobedient for a while as a test, but He is ever watchful of their actions and is swift in His punishment.

89:15-16. Human beings are sometimes tested through ease and comfort (v.15), and sometimes through difficulties and hardships (v.16). An ungrateful person complains and regards his unfortunate situation as a sign of Allāh's pleasure or displeasure. In fact both conditions are a test from Allāh سبحانه وتعالى ; in ease and comfort we must be thankful to Him and generous to our fellow human beings, and during more difficult times, we must be patient and forgiving.

**WE HAVE LEARNED:**

* Many creations of Allāh سبحانه وتعالى stand witness to His power.
* In the past, Allāh سبحانه وتعالى has destroyed many powerful kings and nations for their disobedience.
* Both the comforts and the difficulties of life are a test from Allāh سبحانه وتعالى and they invite the true Believers to show their faith in Allāh's سبحانه وتعالى Mercy.

## VOCABULARY I

### ٨٩- سُورَةُ ٱلْفَجْرِ

| | | |
|---|---|---|
| ١-وَٱلْفَجْرِ | *Wa-(a)l-Fajr(i)* | By the *fajr*, by the dawn |
| ٢-وَلَيَالٍ عَشْرٍ | *Wa-layālin 'ashr(in)* | By the nights ten |
| ٣-وَٱلشَّفْعِ | *Wa-(a)sh-shaf'i* | By the even |
| وَٱلْوَتْرِ | *wa-(a)l-watr(i)* | and the odd |
| ٤-وَٱلَّيْلِ | *Wa-(a)l-lail(i)* | By the night |
| إِذَا يَسْرِ | *'idhā yasr(i)* | when it passes away |
| ٥-هَلْ فِي ذَٰلِكَ | *Hal fī dhālika* | Is there surely in these |
| قَسَمٌ | *qasam(un)* | adjurations, oath |
| لِّذِى حِجْرٍ | *li-dhī ḥijr(in)* | for a thinking person |
| ٦-أَلَمْ تَرَ كَيْفَ | *'Alam tara kaifa* | Do you not see how, |
| فَعَلَ رَبُّكَ | *fa'ala Rabbu-ka* | did your Lord |
| بِعَادٍ | *bi-'ād(in)* | with *'Ād* (people) |

| | | |
|---|---|---|
| ٧-إِرَمَ | *'Irama* | The city of *Iram* |
| ذَاتِ ٱلْعِمَادِ | *dhāti-(a)l-'imād(i)* | with lofty pillars |
| ٨-الَّتِى | *'Allatī* | Of which |
| لَمْ يُخْلَقْ | *lam yukhlaq* | was not created |
| مِثْلُهَا | *mithlu-hā* | like it |
| فِى ٱلْبِلَٰدِ | *fi-(a)l-bilād(i)* | in the lands, in the cities |
| ٩-وَثَمُودَ ٱلَّذِينَ | *Wa-Thamūda-(a)l-ladhīna* | And (people ) of *Thamūd* who |
| جَابُوا ٱلصَّخْرَ | *jābu-(a)ṣ-ṣakhra* | cut out the rocks |
| بِٱلْوَادِ | *bi-(a)l-wād(i)* | in the valley |
| ١٠-وَفِرْعَوْنَ | *Wa-Fir'awna* | And Pharaoh |
| ذِى ٱلْأَوْتَادِ | *dhi -(a)l-'awtād(i)* | The lord of stakes, the powerful |
| ١١-الَّذِينَ طَغَوْا | *'Alladhīna ṭaghaw* | Those who transgressed |
| فِي ٱلبِلَٰدِ | *fi-(a)l-bilād(i)* | in the lands |
| ١٢-فَأَكْثَرُوا | *Fa-'aktharū* | And multiplied, |
| فِيهَا الْفَسَادَ | *fī-hā-(a)l-fasād(a)* | in it the iniquity, the mischief |
| ١٣-فَصَبَّ عَلَيْهِمْ | *Fa-ṣabba 'alai-him* | Therefore poured on them |
| رَبُّكَ | *Rabbu-ka* | your Lord |
| سَوطَ عَذَابٍ | *sawṭa 'adhāb(in)* | disaster of punishment |
| ١٤-إِنَّ رَبَّكَ | *'Inna Rabba-ka* | For your Lord |
| لَبِٱلْمِرْصَادِ | *la-bi-(a)l-mirṣād(i)* | is on a watch-tower, ever watchful |
| ١٥-فَأَمَّا ٱلْانسَٰنُ | *Fa-'amma-(a)l-'insān(u)* | Now, as for the man, as for humankind |
| إِذَا مَا ابْتَلَٰهُ | *'idhā ma-(a)btalā-hu* | when (He) tries him |
| رَبُّهُ | *Rabbu-hū* | his Lord |

| | | |
|---|---|---|
| فَأَكْرَمَهُ | *fa-'akrama-hū* | so honoring him |
| وَنَعَّمَهُ | *wa-na''ama-hū* | and blessing him |
| فَيَقُولُ | *fa-yaqūlu* | so says he |
| رَبِّى أَكْرَمَنِ | *Rabbī 'akraman(i)* | my Lord honored me |
| ١٦-وَأَمَّآ إِذَا | *Wa-'amma 'idhā* | And when |
| مَا ٱبْتَلَٰهُ | *mā '(a)btalā-hu* | He tries him |
| فَقَدَرَ عَلَيْهِ | *fa-qadara 'alai-hi* | straightening for him, restricting |
| رِزْقَهُ | *rizqa-hū* | his subsistence, means |
| فَيَقُولُ | *fa-yaqūlu* | so he says |
| رَبِّىَ أَهَٰنَنِ | *Rabbī 'ahānan(i)* | my Lord has despised me, humiliated me |

*Lesson 4*

# *AL-FAJR, 89:17-30*

## THE BREAK OF DAY / THE DAWN

### Revealed in Makkah

---

| **TRANSLITERATION**: | **ARABIC TEXT**: |
|---|---|
| 17. *Kallā bal-lā-tukrimūna-(a)l-yatīm(a)* | -كَلَّا بَل لَّا تُكْرِمُونَ الْيَتِيمَ ۝ |
| 18. *Wa lā-taḥāḍḍūna 'alā ṭa'āmi-(a)l-miskīn(i)* | -وَلَا تَحَاضُّونَ عَلَىٰ طَعَامِ الْمِسْكِينِ ۝ |
| 19. *Wa ta'kulūna-(a)t-turātha 'akla-(a)l-lammā(n)* | -وَتَأْكُلُونَ التُّرَاثَ أَكْلًا لَّمًّا ۝ |
| 20. *Wa tuḥibbūna-(a)l-māla ḥubban jammā(n)* | -وَتُحِبُّونَ الْمَالَ حُبًّا جَمًّا ۝ |
| 21. *Kallā 'idhā dukkati-(a)l-'arḍu dakkan dakkā(n)* | -كَلَّا إِذَا دُكَّتِ الْأَرْضُ دَكًّا دَكًّا ۝ |
| 22. *Wa jā'a Rabbu-ka wa-(a)l-malaku ṣaffan ṣaffā(n)* | -وَجَاءَ رَبُّكَ وَالْمَلَكُ صَفًّا صَفًّا ۝ |
| 23. *Wa jī'a yawma'idhin bi-jahannam(a)* | -وَجِيءَ يَوْمَئِذٍ بِجَهَنَّمَ ۚ |
| *yawma'idhin yatadhakkaru-(a)l-'insānu* | يَوْمَئِذٍ يَتَذَكَّرُ الْإِنسَانُ |
| *wa 'annā la-hu-(a)dh-dhikrā* | وَأَنَّىٰ لَهُ الذِّكْرَىٰ ۝ |
| 24. *Yaqūlu yā laitanī qaddamtu li-ḥayātī* | -يَقُولُ يَا لَيْتَنِي قَدَّمْتُ لِحَيَاتِي ۝ |
| 25. *Fa-yawma'idhin lā yu'adhdhibu 'adhāba-hū 'aḥad(un)* | -فَيَوْمَئِذٍ لَّا يُعَذِّبُ عَذَابَهُ أَحَدٌ ۝ |
| 26. *Wa lā yūthiqu wathāqa-hū 'aḥad(un)* | -وَلَا يُوثِقُ وَثَاقَهُ أَحَدٌ ۝ |
| 27. *Yā'ayyatuha-(a)n-nafsu-(a)l-muṭma'innah(tu)* | -يَا أَيَّتُهَا النَّفْسُ الْمُطْمَئِنَّةُ ۝ |
| 28. *'Irji'ī 'ilā Rabbi-ki rāḍiyatan marḍiyyah(tan)* | -ارْجِعِي إِلَىٰ رَبِّكِ رَاضِيَةً مَّرْضِيَّةً ۝ |
| 29. *Fa-(a)dkhulī fī 'ibādī* | -فَادْخُلِي فِي عِبَادِي ۝ |
| 30. *Wa-(a)dkhulī jannatī* | -وَادْخُلِي جَنَّتِي ۝ |

**TRANSLATIONS**:

17. No, no! But you honor
not the orphan!
18. Nor do you encourage one another
to feed the poor!
19. And you devour inheritance
all with greed,
20. And you love wealth with inordinate love!
21. No! When the earth is
pounded to powder,
22. And your Lord comes,
and His angels rank upon rank,
23. And Hell, that Day, is brought (face to face),
on that Day will man remember,
but how will that remembrance
profit him?
24. He will say: "Ah ! Would that I had sent
forth (Good Deeds) for (this) my (Future) Life!"
25. For, that Day, His Chastisement will be such
as none (else) can inflict.
26. And His bonds will be such as none
(other) can bind.
27. (To the righteous soul will be said:)
"O (you) soul, in complete rest and satisfaction!"
28. "Come back you to your Lord,-well pleased
(yourself), and well-pleasing to Him!"
29. "Enter you, then, among My Devotees!"
30. "Yes, enter you My Heaven!"

17. Nay, but you (for your part) honour
not the orphan
18. And urge not on
the feeding of the poor,
19. And you devour heritages with
devouring greed
20. And love wealth with abounding love.
21. Nay, but the earth is
ground to atoms, grinding, grinding,
22. And your Lord shall come
with angels, rank on rank,
23. And hell is brought near
that day; on that day man will remember,
but how will the remembrance
(then avail him)?
24. He will say: Ah, would that I had sent
before me (some provision) for my life!
25. None punishes as He will punish on
that day!
26. None can bind as He then
will bind.
27. But ah!
you soul at peace!
28. Return to your Lord,
content in His good pleasure!
29. Enter you among My bondmen!
30. Enter you My Garden!

---

**EXPLANATION**:

89:17-20. Four evils of Makkan society are recounted in these verses. The orphans (v.16) were not cared for. The poor (v.17) were not fed properly. Inheritance, rights of the weak, the orphans and the minors were not respected. People were very materialistic, and had an abundant love for wealth.

89:21-24. However, all the wealth and power of this world will not suffice such people, and death shall certainly overtake them. On the Day of Judgment, they will regret their actions and will wish to have another chance. However, it will be too late.

89:25-26. The severity of punishment for the criminals that day will be such as no one has seen before. No pain of this world could be compared with the pain the evil soul will suffer that day.

89:27-30. The rewards for the pious soul would also be the greatest. It will be a soul at peace, happy with its Lord and the Lord happy with it. It will join the ranks of the pious among Allāh's servants who will enter the *Jannah* and enjoy its pleasures forever.

**WE HAVE LEARNED**:

* Many powers in the past have been destroyed because of their disobedience to Allāh سبحانه وتعالى .
* They have disregarded the rights of orphans, the needy and the weak in this life.
* In the *'Ākhirah*, full justice will be established, both for the evil-doers and for the righteous.

VOCABULARY II

سُورَةُ الفَجْرِ

| | | |
|---|---|---|
| ١٧-كَلاَّ بَلْ | *Kallā bal* | No, Nay, But |
| لاَّ تُكْرِمُونَ | *lā tukrimūna* | you do not honor |
| اَلْيَتِيمَ | *'al-yatīm(a)* | the orphan |
| ١٨-ولاَ تَحَـٰضُّونَ | *Wa-lā taḥaḍḍūna* | and do not encourage each other |
| عَلَىٰ طَعَامِ | *'alā ṭa'āmi* | to feed, feeding |
| اَلْمِسْكِينِ | *'al-miskīn(i)* | the poor, |
| ١٩-وتَأْكُلُونَ | *Wa-ta'kulūna* | And you devour, and you eat |
| اَلتُّرَاثَ | *'at-turātha* | the inheritance, the heritage |
| أَكْلاً لَّمًّا | *'aklan lammā(n)* | devouring indiscriminately, with greed |

| | | |
|---|---|---|
| ٢٠-وَتُحِبُّونَ | *Wa-tuḥibbūna* | And you love |
| اَلْمَالَ | *'al-māla* | the wealth |
| حُبًّا جَمًّا | *ḥubban jammā(n)* | with great love, with abounding love |
| ٢١-كَلاَّ إِذَا | *Kallā 'idhā* | No, nay when |
| دُكَّتِ ٱلأَرْضُ | *dukkati-(a)l-'arḍu* | ground the Earth to atoms |
| دَكًّا دَكًّا | *dakkan dakkā(n)* | pounded to powder, grinding |
| ٢٢-وَجَآءَ رَبُّكَ | *Wa-jā'a Rabbu-ka* | And comes your Lord |
| وَٱلْمَلَكُ | *wa-(a)l-malaku* | and the angels |
| صَفًّا صَفًّا | *ṣaffan ṣaffā(n)* | rank upon rank |
| ٢٣-وَجِاْىٓءَ | *Wa-jī'a* | And brought near |
| يَوْمَئِذٍ | *yawma'idhin* | on that day |
| بِجَهَنَّمَ | *bi-jahannam(a)* | (is) The Hell |
| يَوْمَئِذٍ | *yawma'idhin* | on that day |
| يَتَذَكَّرُ | *yatadhakkaru* | will remember |
| اَلْإِنسَٰنُ | *'al-'insānu* | the man, humankind |
| وَأَنَّىٰ لَهُ | *wa-'annā la-hu* | and how will (help) to him |
| اَلذِّكْرَىٰ | *'adh-dhikrā* | the remembrance |
| ٢٤-يَقُولُ | *Yaqūlu* | He will say |
| يَٰلَيْتَنِى | *yā-laitanī* | Ah ! would that |
| قَدَّمْتُ | *qaddamtu* | I had sent forth |
| لِحَيَاتِى | *li-ḥayātī* | for my life (of Hereafter) |
| ٢٥-فَيَوْمَئِذٍ | *Fa-yawma'idhin* | For that day |
| لاَّ يُعَذِّبُ | *la yu'adhdhibu* | no one can punish |

| | | |
|---|---|---|
| عَذَابَهُ | *'adhāba-hū* | His punishment |
| أَحَدٌ | *'aḥad(un)* | no one else, anyone |
| ٢٦-وَلَا يُوثِقُ | *Wa-la yūthiqu* | And no one binds |
| وَثَاقَهُ أَحَدٌ | *wathāqa-hu 'aḥad(un)* | His binding as no one else |
| ٢٧-يَٰأَيَّتُهَا ٱلنَّفْسُ | *Ya-'ayyatu-ha-(a)n-nafsu* | O, the soul |
| ٱلْمُطْمَئِنَّةُ | *'al-muṭma'innah(tu)* | at complete rest, at peace |
| ٢٨-ٱرْجِعِيٓ | *'Irji'ī* | Return, come back |
| إِلَىٰ رَبِّكِ | *'ilā Rabbi-ki* | to your Lord |
| رَاضِيَةً مَّرْضِيَّةً | *rāḍiyatan marḍiyyah(tan)* | well pleased and well pleasing (to Him) |
| ٢٩-فَٱدْخُلِي | *Fa-(a)dkhulī* | So, enter |
| فِي عِبَٰدِي | *fī 'ibādī* | among My bondmen, among My devotees |
| ٣٠-وَٱدْخُلِي جَنَّتِي | *Wa-(a)dkhulī jannatī* | And enter My Garden, My *Jannah* |

**Lesson 5**

# AL-GHĀSHIYAH, 88:1-16
## THE OVERWHELMING EVENT / THE OVERWHELMING
### Revealed in Makkah

---

**INTRODUCTION:**

This is an early Makkan *Sūrah*. It describes the separate conditions that both the People of Fire and the People of *Jannah* will find themselves in on the Day of Judgment.

Through evocative descriptions of that Day, man is inspired to think and reflect on Allāh's Majesty and His Infinite Power.

**TRANSLITERATION:**

*Bismillāhi-(a)r-Raḥmāni-(a)r-Raḥīm(i)*

1. *Hal 'atā-ka ḥadīthu-(a)l-ghāshiyah(ti)*

2. *Wujūhun yawma'idhin khāshi'ah(tun)*

3. *'Āmilatu-(a)n-nāṣibah(tun)*

4. *Taṣlā nāran ḥāmiyah(tan)*

5. *Tusqā min 'ainin 'āniyah(tin)*

6. *Laisa la-hum ṭa'āmun 'illā min ḍarī'(in)*

7. *Lā yusminu wa lā yughnī min jū'(in)*

8. *Wujūhun yawma'idhin nā'imah(tun)*

9. *Li-sa'yi-hā rāḍiyah(tun)*

10. *Fī jannatin 'āliyah(tin)*

**ARABIC TEXT:**

بِسْمِ اللهِ الرَّحْمٰنِ الرَّحِيْمِ

هَلْ أَتٰىكَ حَدِيْثُ الْغَاشِيَةِ ۝

وُجُوْهٌ يَّوْمَئِذٍ خَاشِعَةٌ ۝

عَامِلَةٌ نَّاصِبَةٌ ۝

تَصْلٰى نَارًا حَامِيَةً ۝

تُسْقٰى مِنْ عَيْنٍ اٰنِيَةٍ ۝

لَيْسَ لَهُمْ طَعَامٌ اِلَّا مِنْ ضَرِيْعٍ ۝

لَا يُسْمِنُ وَلَا يُغْنِيْ مِنْ جُوْعٍ ۝

وُجُوْهٌ يَّوْمَئِذٍ نَّاعِمَةٌ ۝

لِّسَعْيِهَا رَاضِيَةٌ ۝

فِيْ جَنَّةٍ عَالِيَةٍ ۝

11. *Lā tasma'u fī-hā lāghiyah(tan)* — -لَّا تَسْمَعُ فِيهَا لَاغِيَةً ۝

12. *Fī-hā 'ainun jāriyah(tun)* — -فِيهَا عَيْنٌ جَارِيَةٌ ۝

13. *Fī-hā sururun marfū'ah(tun)* — -فِيهَا سُرُرٌ مَّرْفُوعَةٌ ۝

14. *Wa 'akwābun mawdū'ah(tun)* — -وَأَكْوَابٌ مَّوْضُوعَةٌ ۝

15. *Wa namāriqu masfūfah(tun)* — -وَنَمَارِقُ مَصْفُوفَةٌ ۝

16. *Wa zarābiyyu mabthūthah(tun)* — -وَزَرَابِيُّ مَبْثُوثَةٌ ۝

**TRANSLATIONS:**

In the name of Allāh, Most Gracious,
Most Merciful.

1. Has the story reached you,
   of the Overwhelming (Event)?
2. Some faces, that Day,
   will be humiliated,
3. Labouring (hard), weary,
4. The while they enter the Blazing Fire,
5. The while they are given, to drink,
   of a boiling hot spring,
6. No food will there be for them
   but a bitter *Ḍārī'*
7. Which will neither nourish
   nor satisfy hunger.
8. (Other) faces that Day will be joyful,
9. Pleased with their Striving,
10. In a Garden on high,
11. Where they shall hear no (word) of vanity:
12. In it will be a bubbling spring:
13. In it will be Thrones (of dignity),
    raised on high,
14. Goblets placed (ready),
15. And Cushions set in rows,

In the name of Allāh, the Beneficent,
the Merciful.

1. Has there come to you tidings
   of the Overwhelming?
2. On that day (many) faces
   will be downcast,
3. Toiling, weary,
4. Scorched by burning fire,
5. Drinking from a
   boiling spring,
6. No food for them
   save bitter thorn fruit
7. Which does not nourish
   nor release from hunger.
8. On that day other faces will be calm,
9. Glad for their effort past,
10. In a high garden
11. Where they hear no idle speech,
12. Wherein is a gushing spring,
13. Wherein are couches
    raised,
14. And goblets set at hand
15. And cushions ranged

16. And rich carpets (all) spread out.

16. And silken carpets spread.

**EXPLANATION:**

88:1. The news of the Overwhelming and Overshadowing Event, *'Al-Ghāshiyah*, refers to the Day of Judgment.

88:2-7. The Day of Judgment will be a harsh Day for the disobedient and the arrogant. The faces of the disbelievers on that Day will be gloomy, down cast, humiliated, laboring and weary (v. 2-3). The burning fire of Hell will make them thirsty, but there will only be boiling water to drink. The toil of the Day will make them hungry, yet they will have only the thorny plant of *Ḍarī'* to eat. The water will not quench their thirst nor will the food satisfy their hunger.

88:8-16. On this Day, the believers will be in sharp contrast to the non-believers. Their faces will reflect the joy and calm of their past righteous deeds. They will enjoy the beauty of *Jannah,* in gardens high with cool bubbling springs.

The people of *Jannah* will sit happily on thrones raised high, reclining on cushions, with carpets of welcome spread; drinking from ornate goblets and conversing pleasantly with one another.

This graphic description of the joys of *Jannah* tries to make us comprehend them with our limited senses and experiences. The pleasures of *Jannah* are such that they cannot be described through ordinary speech or explained for simple human understanding.

**WE HAVE LEARNED:**

* The overwhelming event is the day of *Qiyāmah.*
* On that Day the faces of the wicked will be down cast and in humiliation.
* The faces of the Righteous will be joyful and glowing.

## VOCABULARY I

### ٨٨- سُورَةُ ٱلْغَاشِيَةِ

| | | |
|---|---|---|
| ١-هَلْ أَتَـٰكَ | *Hal 'atā-ka* | Has come to you |
| حَدِيثُ ٱلْغَـٰشِيَةِ | *ḥadīthu-(a)l-Ghāshiyah(ti)* | the story of the Tidings of Overwhelming |
| ٢-وُجُوهٌ يَوْمَئِذٍ | *Wujūhun yawma'idhin* | Some faces that day |
| خَـٰشِعَةٌ | *khāshi'ah(tun)* | will be humiliated, will be downcast |
| ٣-عَامِلَةٌ | *'Āmilah(tun)* | Laboring hard |
| نَّاصِبَةٌ | *nāṣibah(tun)* | weary |
| ٤-تَصْلَىٰ | *Taṣlā* | Scorched (by) |
| نَاراً حَامِيَةً | *nāran ḥāmiyah(tan)* | a fire blazing, burning |
| ٥-تُسْقَىٰ | *Tusqā* | They are given drinking |
| مِنْ عَيْنٍ | *min 'ain(in)* | from spring |
| ءَانِيَةٍ | *'āniyah(tin)* | boiling hot |
| ٦-لَّيْسَ لَهُمْ | *Laisa la-hum* | There is nothing for them |
| طَعَامٌ | *ṭa'ām(un)* | food |
| إِلاَّ مِن ضَرِيعٍ | *'illā min ḍarī'(in)* | except from thorn grass |
| ٧-لاَّ يُسْمِنُ | *Lā yusminu* | Which does not nourish |
| وَلاَ يُغْنِى | *wa-lā-yughnī* | and does not satisfy |
| مِنْ جُوعٍ | *min jū'(in)* | from hunger |
| ٨-وُجُوهٌ | *Wujūh(un)* | (other) faces |
| يَوْمَئِذٍ | *yawma'idhin* | on that day |
| نَّاعِمَةٌ | *nā'imah(tun)* | (will be) happy |
| ٩-لِسَعْيِهَا | *Li-sa'yi-hā* | For their effort, striving |

| | | |
|---|---|---|
| رَاضِيَةٌ | *rāḍiyah(tun)* | pleased, happy |
| ١٠-فِي جَنَّةٍ | *fī jannat(in)* | in a Garden |
| عَالِيَةٍ | *'āliyah(tin)* | high |
| ١١-لاَّ تَسْمَعُ | *Lā tasma'u* | they do not hear |
| فِيْهَا لَـٰغِيَةً | *Fī-hā lāghiyah(tan)* | in it speech of vanity, idle speech |
| ١٢-فِيهَا عَينٌ | *Fī-hā 'ain(un)* | In it there is a spring |
| جَارِيَةٌ | *jāriyah(tun)* | bubbling, |
| ١٣-فِيهَا سُرُرٌ | *Fī-hā sururun* | In it are thrones, couches |
| مَّرْفُوعَةٌ | *marfū'ah(tun)* | raised on high |
| ١٤-وَأَكْوَابٌ | *Wa-'akwāb(un)* | And goblets |
| مَّوْضُوعَةٌ | *mawḍū'ah(tun)* | set at hand, placed ( ready) |
| ١٥-وَنَمَارِقُ | *Wa-namāriqu* | And cushions |
| مَصْفُوفَةٌ | *maṣfūfah(tun)* | set in row, arranged |
| ١٦-وَزَرَابِيُّ | *Wa-zarābiyyu* | Rich silken carpets |
| مَبْثُوثَةٌ | *mabthūtha(tun)* | spread out |

*Lesson 6*

# *AL-GHĀSHIYAH, 88:17-26*

## THE OVERWHELMING EVENT / THE OVERWHELMING

**Revealed in Makkah**

| **TRANSLITERATION:** | **ARABIC TEXT:** |
|---|---|
| 17. *'Afalā yanẓurūna 'ila-(a)l-'ibili kaifa khuliqat* | أَفَلَا يَنظُرُونَ إِلَى ٱلْإِبِلِ كَيْفَ خُلِقَتْ ۝ - |
| 18. *Wa 'ila-(a)s-samā'i kaifa rufi'at* | وَإِلَى ٱلسَّمَآءِ كَيْفَ رُفِعَتْ ۝ - |
| 19. *Wa 'ila-(a)l-jibāli kaifa nuṣibat* | وَإِلَى ٱلْجِبَالِ كَيْفَ نُصِبَتْ ۝ - |
| 20. *Wa 'ila-(a)l-'arḍi kaifa suṭiḥat* | وَإِلَى ٱلْأَرْضِ كَيْفَ سُطِحَتْ ۝ - |
| 21. *Fa-dhakkir 'innamā 'anta mudhakkir(un)* | فَذَكِّرْ إِنَّمَآ أَنتَ مُذَكِّرٌ ۝ - |
| 22. *Lasta 'alai-him bi-musaiṭir(in)* | لَّسْتَ عَلَيْهِم بِمُصَيْطِرٍ ۝ - |
| 23. *'Illā man tawallā wa kafar(a)* | إِلَّا مَن تَوَلَّىٰ وَكَفَرَ ۝ - |
| 24. *Fa-yu'adhdhibu-hu-(A)llāhu-(a)l-'adhāba-(a)l-'akbar(a)* | فَيُعَذِّبُهُ ٱللَّهُ ٱلْعَذَابَ ٱلْأَكْبَرَ ۝ - |
| 25. *'Inna 'ilai-nā 'iyāba-hum* | إِنَّ إِلَيْنَآ إِيَابَهُمْ ۝ - |
| 26. *Thumma 'inna 'alai-nā ḥisāba-hum* | ثُمَّ إِنَّ عَلَيْنَا حِسَابَهُم ۝ - |

**TRANSLATIONS:**

17. Do they not look at the Camels, how they are made?
18. And at the Sky, how it is raised high?
19. And at the mountains, how they are fixed firm?
20. And at the Earth, how it is spread out?

17. Will they not regard the camels how they are created?
18. And the heaven, how it is raised?
19. And the hills, how they are set up?
20. And the earth, how it is spread?

21. Therefore do you give admonition,
for you are one to admonish.
22. You are not one to manage
(men's) affairs.
23. But if any turn away and reject Allāh,
24. Allāh will punish him with
a mighty Punishment.
25. For to Us will be their Return;
26. Then it will be for Us
to call them to account.

21. Remind them,
for you are but a remembrancer,
22. You are not at all a warder
over them.
23. But whoso is averse and disbelieves,
24. Allāh will punish him with
direst punishment.
25. Lo! to Us is their return
26. And Ours
their reckoning.

---

**EXPLANATION**:

88:17-20. These verses describe the power of Allāh سبحانه وتعالى. The camel is the most useful animal for the Bedouin. It can travel long distances with little water, and is able to survive on small, sparse shrubs found in the desert. It is a constant companion of the Bedouin.

The sky, the mountains and the earth are a familiar environment for every human being. Allāh سبحانه وتعالى stresses in these verses that human existence is not possible without the life-giving interactions of these special creations of Allāh سبحانه وتعالى. These creations indicate the plan of a Wise Creator, and testify to His powers of creation.

88:21-26. Most of the *Kuffār*, in spite of all the signs of the Heavens and the Earth, were not prepared to accept the existence of Allāh سبحانه وتعالى or the concept of Resurrection on the Day of Judgment. Some who accepted Allah associated Him with other gods and goddesses. In these verses, Rasūlullāh ﷺ is advised to remind them about the Day of Judgment; the hardships the *Kuffār* will face, and the pleasures the believers will experience. While we are alive, there is time for us to repent and accept the truth. After death, there is no returning and no repenting.

The role of Rasūlullāh ﷺ as a believer was to offer the Message and to remind the people of the consequences of disbelief. He did not use forceful means. Guidance lies in the hand of Allāh سبحانه وتعالى, to whom all will return for Judgment.

**WE HAVE LEARNED**:

* The Qur'ān is a reminder, teaching us what to follow and what to avoid.
* We have no power over other people, and no more responsibility except to give them the message of Allāh سبحانه وتعالى .
* Finally we all shall return to Allāh سبحانه وتعالى who will judge us according to our deeds.

| | | |
|---|---|---|
| ١٧-أَفَلَا يَنْظُرُونَ | *'A-falā yanẓurūna* | Do they not look, regard |
| إِلَى ٱلْإِبِلِ | *'ila-(a)l-'ibili* | at the camels |
| كَيْفَ خُلِقَتْ | *kaifa khuliqat* | how are they created |
| ١٨-وَإِلَى ٱلسَّمَاءِ | *Wa-'ila (a)s-samā'i* | And at the sky, the Heaven |
| كَيْفَ رُفِعَتْ | *kaifa rufi'at* | how it is raised |
| ١٩-وَإِلَى ٱلْجِبَالِ | *Wa-'ila-(a)l-jibāli* | And at the mountains |
| كَيْفَ نُصِبَتْ | *kaifa nuṣibat* | how they are fixed firm |
| ٢٠-وَإِلَى ٱلْأَرْضِ | *Wa-'ila-(a)l-'arḍi* | And at the Earth |
| كَيْفَ سُطِحَتْ | *kaifa suṭiḥat* | how it is spread out |
| ٢١-فَذَكِّرْ | *Fa-dhakkir* | Therefore, remind (them) |
| إِنَّمَآ أَنْتَ | *'inna-mā 'anta* | you are only |
| مُذَكِّرٌ | *mudhakkir(un)* | one to remind, remembrancer |
| ٢٢-لَّسْتَ عَلَيْهِمْ | *Lasta 'alai-him* | you are not on them |
| بِمُصَيْطِرٍ | *bi-muṣaiṭir(in)* | a manager of affairs, a warder |
| ٢٣-إِلَّا مَنْ تَوَلَّىٰ | *'Illa man tawallā* | But who sees averse, who turns away |
| وَكَفَرَ | *wa-kafara* | and disbelieves |
| ٢٤-فَيُعَذِّبُهُ | *Fa-yu'adhdhibu-hu* | Surely will punish him |
| ٱللَّهُ | *'Allāh(u)* | Allah |
| ٱلْعَذَابَ ٱلْأَكْبَرَ | *'al-'adhāba-(a)l-'akbar(a)* | the greatest punishment |
| ٢٥-إِنَّ إِلَيْنَآ | *'Inna 'ilai-nā* | For to Us, Indeed unto Us |
| إِيَابَهُمْ | *'iyāba-hum* | their return |
| ٢٦-ثُمَّ إِنَّ | *Thumma 'inna* | Then surely |
| عَلَيْنَا حِسَابَهُم | *'alai-nā ḥisāba-hum* | for Us is their accounting |

Lesson 7

سورة الأعلى — آياتها ١٩ — ترتيبها ٨٧

# *AL-'A'LĀ, 87:1-8*

## THE MOST HIGH / THE MOST HIGH

**Revealed in Makkah**

---

**INTRODUCTION:**

This is one of the earliest Makkan *Suwar*. According to some reliable commentators, it is eighth in the chronological order of revelation.

This *Sūrah* describes Allāh's power of creation, support and guidance. It also deals with human potential of an ordered and gradual progress to a spiritual path of purity and perfection.

| **TRANSLITERATION:** | **ARABIC TEXT:** |
|---|---|
| *Bismillāhi-(a)r-Raḥmāni-(a)r-Raḥīm(i)* | بِسْمِ اللَّهِ الرَّحْمَٰنِ الرَّحِيمِ |
| 1. *Sabbiḥi-'(i)sma Rabbi-ka-(a)l-'a'lā* | -سَبِّحِ اسْمَ رَبِّكَ الْأَعْلَى ○ |
| 2. *'Alladhī khalaqa fa-sawwā* | -الَّذِي خَلَقَ فَسَوَّىٰ ○ |
| 3. *Wa-(a)lladhī qaddara fa-hadā* | -وَالَّذِي قَدَّرَ فَهَدَىٰ ○ |
| 4. *Wa-(a)lladhī 'akhraja-(a)l-mar'ā* | -وَالَّذِي أَخْرَجَ الْمَرْعَىٰ ○ |
| 5. *Fa-ja'ala-hū ghuthā'an 'aḥwā* | -فَجَعَلَهُ غُثَاءً أَحْوَىٰ ○ |
| 6. *Sa-nuqri'u-ka fa-lā tansā* | -سَنُقْرِئُكَ فَلَا تَنسَىٰ ○ |
| 7. *'Illa mā shā''Allāhu 'inna-hū* | -إِلَّا مَا شَاءَ اللَّهُ إِنَّهُ |
| *ya'lamu-(a)l-jahra wa mā yakhfā* | يَعْلَمُ الْجَهْرَ وَمَا يَخْفَىٰ ○ |
| 8. *Wa nuyassiru-ka li-(a)l-yusrā* | -وَنُيَسِّرُكَ لِلْيُسْرَىٰ ○ |

## TRANSLATIONS:

In the name of Allāh, Most Gracious, Most Merciful.

1. Glorify the name of your Guardian-Lord Most High,
2. Who had created, and further, given order and proportion;
3. Who had ordained laws. and granted guidance;
4. And who brings out the (green and luscious) pasture;
5. And then makes it (but) swarthy stubble.
6. By degrees shall We teach you to declare (the Message), so you shall not forget,
7. Except as God wills: For He knows what is manifest and what is hidden.
8. And We will make it easy for you (to follow) the simple (Path).

In the name of Allāh, the Beneficent, the Merciful.

1. Praise the name of your Lord the Most High,
2. Who creates, then disposes;
3. Who measures, then guides;
4. Who brings forth the pasturage,
5. Then turns it to russet stubble.
6. We shall make you read (O' Muhammad) so that you shall not forget,
7. Save that which Allāh wills. Lo! He knows the disclosed and which still is hidden;
8. And We shall ease your way to the state of ease.

---

## EXPLANATION:

87:1-3. These verses glorify Allāh ﷻ , Who is *Rabb*, the Creator and Sustainer of all. He has created everything in due proportion. Allāh's creation has an order and plan. Nothing He has created is in vain. He guides all things on a set path pre-determined by Him. He has provided guidance for human beings, but has granted them the power to choose between good and evil and to judge right from wrong.

87:4-5. Allāh ﷻ has determined a natural law for His creations. He brings forth green pastures from the dead, and then turns these pastures into stubble and straw. This process of birth and decay is repeated in cycles. For the believer, it is sufficient proof of the power that Allāh ﷻ has over birth, death and Resurrection on the Day of Judgment.

87:6. Rasūlullāh ﷺ had been naturally anxious to remember the Message and deliver it exactly as it had been revealed to him. Allāh ﷻ assures him that He, Himself, would teach him the Message in stages, and would ensure that he would not forget it. Thus, the Qur'ān was revealed in stages, to make its memorization, understanding and application to our daily lives easier for us.

87:7-8. Everything in the Universe is according to the commands of Allāh . When a person succeeds at any task, he does so only with His permission. Allāh knows everything, open or hidden (v. 7). Allāh , Who possesses infinite power, promised to guide Rasūlullāh and his followers on the path of Islam, and to make it easy for them to follow it. Allāh has given the believers a faith that will reward them, even if they must face difficulties.

**<u>WE HAVE LEARNED</u>:**

* Allāh has created every thing in due proportion.
* He created laws and guided every one to follow the laws.
* Allāh makes the path of Islam easy, for the Believers, to follow.

## VOCABULARY

### ٨٧-سُورَةُ ٱلأَعْلَىٰ

| | | |
|---|---|---|
| ١-سَبِّحِ ٱسْمَ | *Sabbiḥi-(i)sma* | Glorify the name |
| رَبِّكَ ٱلأَعْلَى | *Rabbi-ka-(a)l-'A'lā* | ( of) your Lord, Most-high |
| ٢-ٱلَّذِى خَلَقَ | *'Alladhī khalaqa* | He Who has created |
| فَسَوَّىٰ | *Fa-sawwā* | then He has given proportion |
| ٣-وَٱلَّذِى قَدَّرَ | *Wa-(a)lladhī qaddara* | And Who ordained law |
| فَهَدَىٰ | *Fa-hadā* | and Who guides |
| ٤-وَٱلَّذِىٓ أَخْرَجَ | *Wa-(a)lladhī 'akhraja* | Who brings out |
| ٱلْمَرْعَىٰ | *'al-mar'ā* | the pasture |
| ٥-فَجَعَلَهُۥ | *Fa-ja'ala-hū* | Then makes it |
| غُثَآءً أَحْوَىٰ | *ghuthā'an 'aḥwa* | swarthy stubble, russet stubble |
| ٦-سَنُقْرِئُكَ | *Sa-Nuqri'u-ka* | We shall make you read |
| فَلَا تَنسَىٰٓ | *fa-lā tansā* | so you shall not forget |
| ٧-إِلَّا | *'Illā* | Except |

| | | |
|---|---|---|
| مَا شَآءَ ٱللَّهُ | *mā sha' 'Allāh(u)* | as Allah Wills |
| إِنَّهُ يَعْلَمُ | *'Inna-hū ya'lamu* | Indeed He knows |
| ٱلْجَهْرَ | *'al-jahra* | what is manifest |
| وَمَا يَخْفَىٰ | *wa-mā yakhfā* | and what is hidden |
| ٨-وَنُيَسِّرُكَ | *Wa-Nuyassiru-ka* | And We shall make it easy |
| لِلْيُسْرَىٰ | *li-(a)l-yusrā* | the path of ease |

*Lesson 8*

## *AL-'A'LĀ, 87:9-19*

### THE MOST HIGH / THE MOST HIGH

**Revealed in Makkah**

---

| **TRANSLITERATION:** | **ARABIC TEXT:** |
|---|---|
| 9. *Fa-dhakkir in-nafa'ati-(a)dh-dhikrā* | فَذَكِّرْ إِنْ نَفَعَتِ الذِّكْرٰى ۝ - |
| 10. *Sa-yadh-dhakkaru man yakhshā* | سَيَذَّكَّرُ مَنْ يَّخْشٰى ۝ - |
| 11. *Wa yatajannabu-ha-(a)l-'ashqā* | وَيَتَجَنَّبُهَا الْأَشْقَى ۝ - |
| 12. *'Al-ladhī yaṣla-(a)n-nāra-(a)l-kubrā* | الَّذِىْ يَصْلَى النَّارَ الْكُبْرٰى ۝ - |
| 13. *Thumma lā yamūtu fī-hā wa lā yaḥyā* | ثُمَّ لَا يَمُوْتُ فِيْهَا وَلَا يَحْيٰى ۝ - |
| 14. *Qad 'aflaḥa man tazakkā* | قَدْ أَفْلَحَ مَنْ تَزَكّٰى ۝ - |
| 15. *Wa dhakara-(i)sma Rabbi-hī fa-ṣallā* | وَذَكَرَ اسْمَ رَبِّهٖ فَصَلّٰى ۝ - |
| 16. *Bal tu'thirūna-(a)l-ḥayāt-ad-dunyā* | بَلْ تُؤْثِرُوْنَ الْحَيٰوةَ الدُّنْيَا ۝ - |
| 17. *Wa-(a)l-'ākhiratu khairun wa 'abqā* | وَالْاٰخِرَةُ خَيْرٌ وَّأَبْقٰى ۝ - |
| 18. *'Inna hādha lafi-(a)ṣ-ṣuḥufi-(a)l-'ūlā* | إِنَّ هٰذَا لَفِى الصُّحُفِ الْأُوْلٰى ۝ - |
| 19. *Ṣuḥufi 'Ibrāhīma wa Mūsā* | صُحُفِ إِبْرٰهِيْمَ وَمُوْسٰى ۝ - |

**TRANSLATIONS:**

9. Therefore give admonition in case the admonition profits (the hearer).
10. The admonition will be received by those who fear (Allāh):

9. Therefore remind (men), for of use is the reminder.
10. He will heed who feareth,

11. But it will be avoided
by those most unfortunate ones,
12. Who will enter the Great Fire,
13. In which they will then neither die nor live.
14. But those will prosper
who purify themselves,
15. And glorify the name of their Guardian
Lord and (lift their hearts) in Prayer.
16. No (behold), you prefer
the life of this world;
17. But the Hereafter is better
and more enduring.
18. And this is in the Books
of the earliest (Revelations),
19. The Books of Abraham and Moses.

11. But the most hapless
will flout it,
12. He who will be flung to the great fire
13. Wherein he will neither die nor live.
14. He is successful
who grows,
15. And remembers the name of his
Lord, so prays.
16. But you prefer
the life of the world
17. Although the Hereafter is better
and more lasting.
18. Lo! This is in the
former scrolls,
19. The Books of Abraham and Moses.

**EXPLANATION**:

87:9-10. The role of Rasūlullāh ﷺ as a *Dā'ī* (preacher) was to invite people to the Truth. A *Dā'ī* constantly invites people to follow the Straight Path. Not everyone, however, pays attention to this call. It is heeded by only those who fear and love Allāh ﷻ.

87:11-13. The non-believer avoids the message and refutes the Truth. His place will be in the Hell-Fire. This existence will be a strange combination of life and death. A disbeliever will neither live, nor will he die in it, but will continue to suffer a tremendous pain that cannot be compared to any known experience.

87:14-15. The Divine Law for the success of man calls for him to believe and to purify his soul. Remembering the name of our Lord and recognizing His presence in our lives at all times is one form of purification. To offer the prescribed prayers and to supplicate to Him for all our needs is another way of reaching Him and purifying ourselves.

87:16-19. The rewards of the *'Ākhirah* are often hidden from human beings but the pleasures of this world are visible and are open to our sensual experiences. Most prefer the transient and temporary pleasures of this world over the permanent and abiding rewards of the Hereafter (v.16-17). The message of Islam was not revealed as a new concept to Rasūlullāh ﷺ; it is the same message which had come to all the Prophets. It had been revealed in all the ancient scriptures, including the *Ṣuḥuf* of Ibrāhīm and the *Tawrāt*, the Book revealed to Mūsā.

Allāh is Glorified, Who has created everything in due order and proportion. Everything works according to His Divine plan. Mankind has been given some degree of freedom to choose between good and evil.

**WE HAVE LEARNED:**

* Muslims have a responsibility to invite others to Islam, and never stop to remind them.
* The separate paths of success and failure have been clearly distinguished from the time of creation, through Divine Revelations.
* The path of success is made clear to those who heed Allāh's Revelations.

## VOCABULARY

### ٨٧-سُورَةُ آلأَعْلَىٰ

| | | |
|---|---|---|
| ٩-فَذَكِّرْ إِن نَّفَعَتِ | *Fa-dhakkir 'in nafa'ati* | Therefore, give admonition in case it profits |
| اَلذِّكْرَىٰ | *'adh-dhikrā* | reminding, admonition |
| ١٠-سَيَذَّكَّرُ | *Sa-yadhdhakkaru* | He will receive admonition, he will heed |
| مَن يَخْشَىٰ | *man yakhshā* | who fears |
| ١١-وَيَتَجَنَّبُهَا | *Wa-yatajannabu-hā* | It will be avoided (by) |
| اَلأَشْقَىٰ | *'al-'ashqā* | the most unfortunate |
| اَلَّذِى يَصْلَىٰ | *'alladhī yaṣlā* | who will burn (into), be exposed to the blaze of |
| اَلنَّارَ آلْكُبْرَىٰ | *'an-nāra-(a)l-kubrā* | the great fire |
| ١٣-ثُمَّ لَا يَمُوتُ | *Thumma lā yamūtu* | Then does not die |
| فِيهَا | fī-hā | in it |
| وَلَا يَحْيَىٰ | *wa-lā yaḥyā* | nor does he live |
| ١٤-قَدْ أَفْلَحَ | *Qad 'aflaḥa* | Surely he is successful |
| مَن تَزَكَّىٰ | *man tazakkā* | who purifies (himself) |

| | | |
|---|---|---|
| ١٥-وَذَكَرَ ٱسْمَ | *Wa-dhakara-(i)sma* | And he remembers the name |
| رَبِّهِۦ فَصَلَّىٰ | *Rabbi-hī fa-ṣallā* | (of) his Lord so offers prayers |
| ١٦-بَلْ تُؤْثِرُونَ | *Bal tu'thirūna* | But you prefer |
| ٱلْحَيَوٰةَ ٱلدُّنْيَا | *'al-ḥayāta-(a)d-dunyā* | the life of this world |
| ١٧-وَٱلْأَخِرَةُ خَيْرٌ | *wa-(a)l'ākhiratu khairun* | And the Hereafter is better |
| وَأَبْقَىٰٓ | *wa-'abqā* | and more lasting |
| ١٨-إِنَّ هَٰذَا | *'inna hādhā* | Indeed this is |
| لَفِى ٱلصُّحُفِ ٱلْأُولَىٰ' | *lafī-(a)ṣ-ṣuḥufi-(a)l-'ūlā* | in the Books of the earliest (Revelations) |
| ١٩-صُحُفِ | *ṣuḥuf(i)* | The Books of |
| إِبْرَٰهِيمَ وَمُوسَىٰ | *'Ibrāhīma wa-Mūsā* | 'Ibrāhīm and Mūsā (Abraham and Moses) |

**Lesson 9**

سُورَةُ الطَّارِقِ

آياتها ١٧ — ترتيبها ٨٦

# *AṬ-ṬĀRIQ, 86:1-17*

## THE NIGHT-VISITANT / THE MORNING STAR

**Revealed in Makkah**

---

**INTRODUCTION:**

This an early Makkan *Sūrah.* The Islamic *Da'wah* was facing stiff opposition at this time, and its success was becoming unnerving to the *Kuffār.* They began to plot against Rasūlullāh ﷺ.

This *Sūrah* deals first with the concept of Resurrection, and then discusses the futility of the *Kuffār's* opposition to the spread of Islam. Allāh سبحانه وتعالى Himself was planning against the plots of the *Kuffār.* Their success in harming Rasūlullāh ﷺ and his followers was short-term, and they were promised Divine punishment in this world and in the Hereafter.

| TRANSLITERATION: | ARABIC TEXT: |
|---|---|
| *Bismillāhi-(a)r-Raḥmāni-(a)r-Raḥīm(i)* | بِسْمِ اللَّهِ الرَّحْمَٰنِ الرَّحِيمِ |
| 1. *Wa-(a)s-samā'i wa-(a)ṭ-ṭāriq(i)* | وَالسَّمَاءِ وَالطَّارِقِ ۝ -١ |
| 2. *Wa mā 'adrā-ka ma-(a)ṭ-ṭāriq(u)* | وَمَا أَدْرَاكَ مَا الطَّارِقُ ۝ -٢ |
| 3. *'An-najmu-(a)th-thāqib(u)* | النَّجْمُ الثَّاقِبُ ۝ -٣ |
| 4. *'In kullu nafsin lammā 'alai-hā ḥāfiẓ(un)* | إِنْ كُلُّ نَفْسٍ لَمَّا عَلَيْهَا حَافِظٌ ۝ -٤ |
| 5. *Fa-l-yanẓuri-(a)l-'insānu mim-ma khuliq(a)* | فَلْيَنْظُرِ الْإِنْسَانُ مِمَّ خُلِقَ ۝ -٥ |
| 6. *Khuliqa min mā'in dāfiq(in)* | خُلِقَ مِنْ مَاءٍ دَافِقٍ ۝ -٦ |
| 7. *Yakhruju min baini-(a)ṣ-ṣulbi wa-(a)t-tarā'ib(i)* | يَخْرُجُ مِنْ بَيْنِ الصُّلْبِ وَالتَّرَائِبِ ۝ -٧ |
| 8. *'Inna-hū 'alā raj'i-hī la-qādir(un)* | إِنَّهُ عَلَىٰ رَجْعِهِ لَقَادِرٌ ۝ -٨ |
| 9. *Yawma tubla-(a)s-sarā'ir(u)* | يَوْمَ تُبْلَى السَّرَائِرُ ۝ -٩ |

| | |
|---|---|
| *10. Fa-mā la-hū min quwwatin wa lā nāṣir(in)* | -فَمَا لَهُ مِنْ قُوَّةٍ وَلَا نَاصِرٍ ۝ |
| *11. Wa-(a)s-samā'i <u>dh</u>āti-(a)r-raj'i* | -وَالسَّمَاءِ ذَاتِ الرَّجْعِ ۝ |
| *12. Wa-(a)l-'arḍi <u>dh</u>āti-(a)ṣ-ṣad'i* | -وَالْأَرْضِ ذَاتِ الصَّدْعِ ۝ |
| *13. 'Inna-hū la-qawlun faṣl(un)* | -إِنَّهُ لَقَوْلٌ فَصْلٌ ۝ |
| *14. Wa mā huwa bi-(a)l-hazl(i)* | -وَمَا هُوَ بِالْهَزْلِ ۝ |
| *15. 'Inna-hum yakīdūna kaidā(n)* | -إِنَّهُمْ يَكِيدُونَ كَيْدًا ۝ |
| *16. Wa 'akīdu kaidā(n)* | -وَأَكِيدُ كَيْدًا ۝ |
| *17. Fa-mahhili-(a)l-kāfirīna 'amhil-hum ruwaida(n)* | -فَمَهِّلِ الْكَافِرِينَ أَمْهِلْهُمْ رُوَيْدًا ۝ |

**<u>TRANSLATIONS</u>:**

In the name of Allāh, Most Gracious,
Most Merciful.

1. By the Sky and the Night-Visitant (in it);
2. And what will explain to you what the Night-Visitant is?
3. (It is) the star of piercing brightness;
4. There is no soul but has a protector over it.
5. Now let man but think from what he is created!
6. He is created from a drop emitted
7. Proceeding from between the backbone and the ribs;
8. Surely (Allāh) is able to bring him back (to Life)!
9. The Day that (all) things secret will be tested,
10. (Man) will have no power, and no helper.

In the name of Allāh, the Beneficent,
the Merciful.

1. By the heaven and the Morning Star
2. Ah, what will tell you what Morning Star is!
3. The piercing Star!
4. No human soul but has a guardian over it.
5. So let man consider from what he is created.
6. He is created from a gushing fluid
7. That issued from between the loins and ribs.
8. Lo! He verily is Able to return him (to life)
9. On the day when hidden thoughts shall be searched out.
10. Then will he have no might nor any helper.

11. By the Firmament
which returns (in its round),
12. And by the Earth which opens out (for the gushing of springs or the sprouting of vegetation)
13. Behold this is the Word
that distinguishes (Good from Evil):
14. It is not a thing for amusement.
15. As for them, they are but plotting
a scheme.
16. And I am planning a scheme.
17. Therefore grant a delay to the unbelievers:
Give respite to them gently
(for a while).

11. By the heaven
which giveth the returning rain,
12. And the earth which splits (with
the growth of trees and plants)
13. Lo! this (Qur'ān) is
a conclusive word,
14. It is no pleasantry.
15. Lo! they plot
a plot (against you, O' Muḥammad)
16. And I plot a plot (against them).
17. So give a respite to the disbelievers.
Deal you gently with them for a
while.

---

**EXPLANATION**:

86:1-4. In these verses, Allāh ﷻ swears by the bright morning star, as a symbol of His power. The cosmic order cannot be held together without a Creator. Allāh ﷻ is the Creator, Protector and Guardian of every human soul.

86:5-8. Allāh ﷻ, the Guardian of the whole cosmic order, is also the Creator of Mankind. He made man from a very humble substance, an invisible drop of semen, which shoots forth from between the back and the ribs. If Allāh ﷻ can create human beings from such an invisible source, He has the power to bring them to life after their death.

86:9-10. On the Day of Judgment, when all hidden things will be made visible; all Power will belong to Allāh ﷻ. None will have power or help besides Allāh ﷻ.

86:11-14. Allāh ﷻ swears by the Heaven, as it sends down rain, and by the Earth, as it splits to bring forth grains and vegetation. These two events cannot occur without a Creator. There is a serious scheme behind this natural phenomenon. Similarly, the Qur'ān is also a serious phenomenon; a Divine Command that distinguishes right from wrong. It is not to be taken lightly.

86:15-17. The Qur'ān speaks about the consequences of disobedience. The plotting of the *Kuffār* is being countered by the planning of Allāh ﷻ Himself. The *Kuffār* have been left to enjoy their temporary success for the time being, which, actually is no success at all.

**WE HAVE LEARNED:**

* All power belongs to Allāh سبحانه وتعالى , the Creator and Sustainer of the Universe.

* The Qur'ān is the final Revelation that distinguishes truth from falsehood.

* The plots of the *Kuffār* against the Muslims will be defeated by Allāh سبحانه وتعالى .

## VOCABULARY

### ٨٦-سُورَةُ ٱلطَّارِق

| | | |
|---|---|---|
| ١-وَٱلسَّمَآءِ | *Wa-(a)s-samā'(i)* | By the sky, Heaven |
| وَٱلطَّارِقِ | *wa-(a)ṭ-ṭāriq(i)* | the Night Visitant, the Morning Star |
| ٢-وَمَا أَدْرَٰكَ | *Wa-mā 'adrā-ka* | And what will explain to you |
| مَا ٱلطَّارِقُ | *mā-'(a)ṭ-ṭāriq(u)* | what the Night Visitant is, what the Morning Star is |
| ٣-اَلنَّجْمُ | *'An-najm(u)* | The Star |
| اَلثَّاقِبُ | *'ath-thāqib(u)* | very bright |
| ٤-إِن كُلُّ نَفْسٍ | *'In kullu nafsin* | For every soul |
| لَّمَّا عَلَيْهَا | *lammā 'alai-hā* | but on it has |
| حَافِظٌ | *ḥāfiẓ(un)* | a protector, guardian |
| ٥-فَلْيَنظُرِ | *Fa-l-yanẓur(i)* | So, let (him) think, look |
| اَلْإِنسَـٰنُ | *'al-'insānu* | the man, humankind |
| مِمَّ خُلِقَ | *mimma khuliq(a)* | from what he was (is) created |
| ٦-خُلِقَ | *Khuliqa* | He was (is) created |
| مِن مَّآءٍ | *min mā'(in)* | from a drop of water |
| دَافِقٍ | *dāfiq(in)* | emitting, gushing |
| ٧-يَخْرُجُ | *Yakhruju* | which proceeds,(it) issuing |
| مِنۢ بَيْنِ ٱلصُّلْبِ | *min baini-(a)ṣ-ṣulbi* | from between the backbone |
| وَٱلتَّرَآئِبِ | *wa-(a)t-tarā'ib(i)* | and the ribs |

| | | |
|---|---|---|
| ٨-إِنَّهُ | *'Inna-Hū* | Surely! He is |
| عَلَىٰ رَجْعِهِ | *'alā raj'i-hī* | on his return (to Him) |
| لَقَادِرٌ | *la-Qādir(un)* | surely is Able |
| ٩-يَوْمَ | *Yawma* | That Day, on the Day |
| تُبْلَىٰ ٱلسَّرَآئِرُ | *tubla-(a)s-sarā'ir(u)* | made manifest the hidden things |
| ١٠-فَمَا لَهُ | *Fa-mā la-hū* | Then, he will have nothing |
| مِن قُوَّةٍ | *min quwwatin* | from power |
| وَلاَ نَاصِرٍ | *wa-lā nāṣir(in)* | and no helper |
| ١١-وَٱلسَّمَآءِ | *wa-(a)s-samā'i* | By the Sky, Heaven |
| ذَاتِ ٱلرَّجْعِ | *dhati-(a)r-raj'i* | which returns, returning rain |
| ١٢-وَٱلأَرْضِ | *Wa-(a)l-'arḍi* | And by the Earth |
| ذَاتِ ٱلصَّدْعِ | *dhāti-(a)ṣ-ṣadi'* | which splits |
| ١٣-إِنَّهُ | *'Inna-hū* | Behold, Indeed it is (Qur'an) |
| لَقَوْلٌ فَصْلٌ | *la-qawlun faṣl(un)* | a Word conclusive, distinguishing |
| ١٤-وَمَا هُوَ | *Wa-mā huwa* | And it is not |
| بِٱلْهَزْلِ | *bi-(a)l-hazl(i)* | for pleasantry, for amusement |
| ١٥-إِنَّهُمْ | *'Inna-hum* | As for them |
| يَكِيدُونَ كَيْداً | *yakīdūna kaida(n)* | they are planning to plot a scheme |
| ١٦-وَأَكِيدُ كَيْداً | *Wa-'akīdu kaida(n)* | And I plot a plot |
| ١٧-فَمَهِّلِ ٱلْكَٰفِرِينَ | *Fa-mahhili-(a)l-kāfirīna* | Therefore, grant delay to the non-believers |
| أَمْهِلْهُمْ | *'amhil-hum* | give them respite, gently |
| رُوَيْداً | *ruwaida(n)* | for a while |

**Lesson 10**

سُورَةُ البُرُوجِ

آياتها ٢٢ — ترتيبها ٨٥

# *AL-BURŪJ, 85:1-10*

## THE ZODIACAL SIGNS / THE MANSIONS OF THE STARS

**Revealed in Makkah**

---

**INTRODUCTION:**

This is an early Makkan *Sūrah*. The *Kuffār* had started persecuting the Muslims and were adopting any means possible to stop the progress of Islam.

In this *Sūrah*, Allāh سُبْحَانَهُ وَتَعَالَىٰ warns the *Kuffār* of the consequences of their evil actions. With a historical reference, He commands the Muslims to follow the example of the earlier believers in showing patience during adversity.

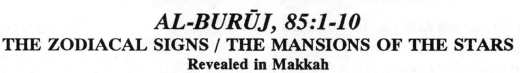

| **TRANSLITERATION:** | **ARABIC TEXT:** |
|---|---|
| *Bismillāhi-(a)r-Raḥmāni-(a)r-Raḥīm(i)* | بِسْمِ اللّٰهِ الرَّحْمٰنِ الرَّحِيْمِ |
| 1. *Wa-(a)s-samā'i dhāti-(a)l-burūj(i)* | -وَالسَّمَآءِ ذَاتِ الْبُرُوْجِ ۝ |
| 2. *Wa-(a)l-yawmi-(a)l-maw'ūd(i)* | -وَالْيَوْمِ الْمَوْعُوْدِ ۝ |
| 3. *Wa shāhidin wa mashhūd(in)* | -وَشَاهِدٍ وَّمَشْهُوْدٍ ۝ |
| 4. *Qutila 'Aṣḥābu-(a)l-'ukhdūd(i)* | -قُتِلَ اَصْحٰبُ الْاُخْدُوْدِ ۝ |
| 5. *'An-nāri dhāti-(a)l-waqūd(i)* | -النَّارِ ذَاتِ الْوَقُوْدِ ۝ |
| 6. *'Idh hum 'alai-hā qu'ūd(un)* | -اِذْ هُمْ عَلَيْهَا قُعُوْدٌ ۝ |
| 7. *Wa hum 'alā mā yaf'alūna* | -وَّهُمْ عَلٰى مَا يَفْعَلُوْنَ |
| *bi-(a)l-mu'minīna shuhūd(un)* | بِالْمُؤْمِنِيْنَ شُهُوْدٌ ۝ |
| 8. *Wa mā naqamū min-hum 'illā an-yu'minū* | -وَمَا نَقَمُوْا مِنْهُمْ اِلَّآ اَنْ يُّؤْمِنُوْا |
| *bi-(A)llāhi-(a)l-'Azīzi-(a)l-Ḥamīd(i)* | بِاللّٰهِ الْعَزِيْزِ الْحَمِيْدِ ۝ |

| | |
|---|---|
| 9. *'Alladhī la-hū mulku-(a)s-samāwāti wa-l-'arḍi* | الَّذِي لَهُ مُلْكُ السَّمٰوٰتِ وَالْأَرْضِ ۚ |
| *wa-(A)llāhu 'alā kulli shai'in shahīd(un)* | وَاللّٰهُ عَلٰى كُلِّ شَيْءٍ شَهِيدٌ ۝ |
| 10. *'Inna-(a)l-ladhīna fatanu-(a)l-mu'minīna wa-(a)l-mu'mināti* | إِنَّ الَّذِينَ فَتَنُوا الْمُؤْمِنِينَ وَالْمُؤْمِنٰتِ |
| *thumma lam yatūbū fa-la-hum 'adhābu jahannama* | ثُمَّ لَمْ يَتُوبُوا فَلَهُمْ عَذَابُ جَهَنَّمَ |
| *wa la-hum 'adhābu-(a)l-ḥarīq(i)* | وَلَهُمْ عَذَابُ الْحَرِيقِ ۝ |

**TRANSLATIONS**:

In the name of Allāh, Most Gracious,
Most Merciful.

1. By the Sky, (displaying) the Zodiacal Signs
2. By the promised Day (of Judgment);
3. By one that witness, and the subject of the witness;
4. Woe to the makers of the pit (of fire),
5. Fire supplied (abundantly) with Fuel.
6. Look! they sat over against the (fire),
7. And they witnessed (all) that they were doing the Believers.
8. And they ill-treated them for no other reason than that they believed in Allāh, Exalted in Power, Worthy of all Praise!
9. Him to Whom belongs the dominion of the heavens and the earth! And Allāh is Witness to all things.
10. Those who persecute (or draw into temptation) the Believers, men and women, and do not turn in repentance, will have the Penalty of Hell; they have the Penalty of the Burning Fire.

In the name of Allāh, the Beneficent,
the Merciful.

1. By the heaven, holding mansions of the stars
2. And by the Promised Day,
3. And by the witness and that whereto he bears testimony,
4. (Self-) destroyed were the owners of the ditch,
5. Of the fuel-fed fire,
6. When they sat by it,
7. And were themselves the witnesses of what they did to the believers.
8. They had naught against them save that they believed in Allāh, the Mighty, Owner of Praise,
9. Him to Whom belongs the Sovereignty of the heavens and the the earth! and Allāh is of all things the Witness.
10. Lo! they who persecute believing men and believing women and repent not, theirs verily will be the doom of hell, and theirs the doom of burning.

**EXPLANATION**:

85:1-3. Allāh سبحانه وتعالى is the Creator of the Heavens, and He will establish the Day of Judgment, at which time He will punish the sinners. On that day Allāh سبحانه وتعالى, His Messengers, His Angels and the Believers will be witnesses against the non-Believers and their wicked deeds. (v.1-3).

85:4-7. In these verses, Allāh سبحانه وتعالى warns of the evil consequences on the Day of Judgment for the *'Aṣḥābu-(a)l-'ukhdūd*, "the Makers of the Pit of Fire" who worked against the Believers. This may refer to some ancient Kings and their courtiers who oppressed the Believers and threw them in the Fire. In general it applies to all the enemies of Islam who oppress and torture the Muslims. On the Day of Judgment those who believed will witness the destruction of their oppressors.

85:8-10. The "Makers of the Fire" tortured the Muslims for no other reason but that they believed in Allāh سبحانه وتعالى, the Owner of Heaven and Earth. Those who persecute innocent Muslims will have their abode in the Fire of Hell; a fitting recompense for those who burned the believers alive and who enjoyed watching their sufferings that they themselves had inflicted upon them.

**WE HAVE LEARNED**:

* On the Day of Judgment Allāh, His Messengers, His Angels and the Believers will be witnesses against the *Kuffār*.
* The Believers many times suffer because of their belief, but ultimately they are successful.
* The non-believers may appear to be successful in this world, but in the end they are the losers.

## VOCABULARY

### ٨٥- سُورَةُ ٱلبُرُوج

| | | |
|---|---|---|
| ١-وَٱلسَّمَآءِ | *Wa-(a)s-samā'i* | By the sky |
| ذَاتِ ٱلْبُرُوجِ | *dhāti-(a)l-burūj(i)* | having Zodiacal signs |
| ٢-وَٱلْيَوْمِ | *Wa-(a)l-yawmi* | And by The Day |
| ٱلْمَوْعُودِ | *'al-maw'ūd(i)* | promised |
| ٣-وَشَاهِدٍ | *Wa-shāhid(in)* | And by the witness |
| وَمَشْهُودٍ | *wa-mashhūd(in)* | and by the subject witnessed |
| ٤-قُتِلَ | *Qutila* | Destroyed, woe to |
| أَصْحَٰبُ ٱلْأُخْدُودِ | *'aṣḥābu -(a)l-'ukhdūd(i)* | the Owners of the Ditch, the Makers of the Pit |

| | | |
|---|---|---|
| ٥-اَلنَّارِ | 'An-nār(i) | the fire |
| ذَاتِ ٱلْوَقُودِ | dhati-(a)l-waqūd(i) | having plenty of fuel |
| ٦-إِذْ هُمْ | 'Idh hum | When, they |
| عَلَيْهَا قُعُودٌ | 'alai-hā qu'ūd(un) | sat on it |
| ٧-وَهُمْ عَلَىٰ | Wa-hum 'alā | And they on |
| مَا يَفْعَلُونَ | mā yaf'alūna | what they were doing |
| بِٱلْمُؤْمِنِينَ | bi-(a)l-mu'minīna | to the Believers |
| شُهُودٌ | shuhūd(un) | witnesses |
| ٨-وَمَانَقَمُوا | Wa-mā naqamū | And they ill treated, took vengence |
| مِنْهُمْ | min-hum | of them |
| إِلَّا أَن يُؤْمِنُوا | 'illa 'an yu'minū | except that they believe |
| بِٱللَّهِ | bi-(A)llāhi | in Allah ﷻ |
| ٱلْعَزِيزِ ٱلْحَمِيدِ | 'al-'Azīzi-(a)l-Ḥamīd(i) | the Mighty, Worthy of Praise |
| ٩-اَلَّذِى لَهُ | 'Alladhī la-hū | He unto Whom belong |
| مُلْكُ ٱلسَّمَوَاتِ | mulku-(a)s-samāwāt(i) | the sovereignty of heavens |
| وَٱلْأَرْضِ | wa-(a)l-'arḍ(i) | and the Earth |
| وَٱللَّهُ | wa-(A)llāhu | and Allah ﷻ is |
| عَلَىٰ كُلِّ شَىْءٍ | 'alā kulli shai'(in) | on everything |
| شَهِيدٌ | shahīd(un) | a witness |
| ١٠-إِنَّ ٱلَّذِينَ | 'Inna '(a)lladhīna | Lo! those who |
| فَتَنُوا | fatanū | persecuted |
| ٱلْمُؤْمِنِينَ | 'al-mu'minīn(a) | the believing men |

| | | |
|---|---|---|
| وَٱلْمُؤْمِنَـٰتِ | *wa-(a)l-mu'mināti* | and the believing women |
| ثُمَّ لَمْ يَتُوبُوا | *thumma lam yatūbū* | then did not repent |
| فَلَهُمْ | *fa-la-hum* | for them is |
| عَذَابُ جَهَنَّمَ | *'adhabu jahannam(a)* | the punishment of Hell |
| وَلَهُمْ | *wa-la-hum* | and for them is |
| عَذَابُ ٱلْحَرِيقِ | *'adhābu-(a)l-ḥarīq(i)* | the punishment of the burning fire |

*Lesson 11*

# *AL-BURŪJ, 85:11-22*

## THE ZODIACAL SIGNS / THE MANSIONS OF THE STARS

**Revealed in Makkah**

---

| **TRANSLITERATION**: | **ARABIC TEXT**: |
|---|---|
| 11. *'Inna-(a)lladhīna 'amanū wa'amilu-(a)ṣ-ṣāliḥāti la-hum* | -إِنَّ الَّذِينَ ءَامَنُوا وَعَمِلُوا الصَّٰلِحَٰتِ لَهُمْ |
| *jannātun tajrī min taḥti-ha-(a)l-'anhāru* | جَنَّٰتٌ تَجْرِى مِن تَحْتِهَا الْأَنْهَٰرُ ۚ |
| *dhālika-(a)l-fawzu-(a)l-kabīr(u)* | ذَٰلِكَ الْفَوْزُ الْكَبِيرُ ۝ |
| 12. *'Inna baṭsha Rabbi-ka la-shadīd(un)* | -إِنَّ بَطْشَ رَبِّكَ لَشَدِيدٌ ۝ |
| 13. *'Inna-Hu Huwa yubdi'u wa yu'īd(u)* | -إِنَّهُۥ هُوَ يُبْدِئُ وَيُعِيدُ ۝ |
| 14. *Wa Huwa-(a)l-Ghafūru-(a)l-Wadūd(u)* | -وَهُوَ الْغَفُورُ الْوَدُودُ ۝ |
| 15. *Dhu-(a)l-'Arshi-(a)l-Majīd(u)* | -ذُو الْعَرْشِ الْمَجِيدُ ۝ |
| 16. *Fa''ālu(n)lli-mā yurīd(u)* | -فَعَّالٌ لِّمَا يُرِيدُ ۝ |
| 17. *Hal 'atā-ka ḥadīthu-(a)l-junūd(i)* | -هَلْ أَتَىٰكَ حَدِيثُ الْجُنُودِ ۝ |
| 18. *Fir'awna wa Thamūd(a)* | -فِرْعَوْنَ وَثَمُودَ ۝ |
| 19. *Bali-(a)l-ladhīna kafarū fī takdhīb(in)* | -بَلِ الَّذِينَ كَفَرُوا فِى تَكْذِيبٍ ۝ |
| 20. *Wa-(A)llāhu min warā'i-him muḥīṭ(un)* | -وَاللَّهُ مِن وَرَآئِهِم مُّحِيطٌ ۝ |
| 21. *Bal huwa Qur'ānun Majīd(un)* | -بَلْ هُوَ قُرْءَانٌ مَّجِيدٌ ۝ |
| 22. *Fī Lawḥin Maḥfūẓ(in)* | -فِى لَوْحٍ مَّحْفُوظٍ ۝ |

**TRANSLATIONS:**

11. For those who believe and do righteous deeds, will be Gardens beneath which Rivers flow. That is the Great Salvation (the fulfillment of all desires),
12. Truly strong is the Grip (and Power) of your Lord.
13. It is He Who creates from the very beginning, and He can restore (life)
14. And He is the Oft-Forgiving, full of loving-Kindness,
15. Lord of the Throne of Glory,
16. Doer (without let) of all that He intends.
17. Has the story reached you, of the Forces
18. Of Pharaoh and the Thamūd?
19. And yet the Unbelievers (persist) in rejecting ( the Truth)!
20. But Allāh does encompass from behind!
21. No, this is a Glorious Qur'ān,
22. (Inscribed) in a Tablet Preserved.

11. Lo! those who believe and do good works, theirs will be Gardens underneath which rivers flow. That is the the Great Success.
12. Lo! the punishment of your Lord is stern.
13. Lo! He it is Who produces, and reproduces,
14. And He is the Forgiving, the Loving
15. Lord of the Throne of Glory,
16. Doer of what He will.
17. Has there come to you the story of the hosts
18. Of the Pharaoh and (the tribe of) Thamūd?
19. Nay, but those who disbelieve live in denial
20. And Allāh, all unseen, surrounds them
21. Nay, but it is a glorious Qur'ān.
22. On a guarded tablet.

---

**EXPLANATION:**

85:11. Those believers who patiently suffered the persecution and pain will also have a fitting recompense for their true faith and righteous actions, the gardens of *Jannah*; under which cool rivers flow. Indeed, that is real and the greatest success.

85:12-16. Allāh سبحانه وتعالى is the Most-Powerful. He is the Creator and Restorer of life (v. 12). He is Forgiving to those who repent, and Kind to those who suffer for their belief in One God (v.14). He is the Lord of the Throne and has the power to do what He wills (v.15-16). He is free to punish the non-believers and to reward the believers in any fashion that pleases Him.

85:17-20. No power on Earth, however great and advanced it may be, can withstand the wrath and anger of Allāh سبحانه وتعالى. The examples of *Fir'awn* and the People of Thamūd testify to their defiance and ultimate destruction. *Fir'awn*, with his powerful army, was drowned chasing the helpless followers of Mūsā عليه السلام. And the People of Thamūd, the builders of a great material civilization, were destroyed by an earthquake. The *Kuffār* of Makkah were no match for *Fir'awn* or the People of Thamūd; and they destroyed themselves through their defiance.

85:21-22. The warnings to the *Kuffār* and the good tidings brought to the believers are delivered through the authentic Book of Allāh سبحانه وتعالى, the Qur'ān, the Glorious, preserved by Allāh سبحانه وتعالى in the *Lawḥ Maḥfūz*, the Guarded Tablets.

**WE HAVE LEARNED:**

* In this *Sūrah* the Qur'ān gives the example of powerful non-believers like *'Aṣḥābu-(a)l-'Ukhdūd*, *Fir'awn* and *Thamūd.*
* Allāh سبحانه وتعالى punished them for their evil deeds and rewarded the believers for the sufferings they endured.
* The promises that Allāh سبحانه وتعالى has made are true for all time.

## VOCABULARY

٨٥- سُورَةُ ٱلْبُرُوجِ

| | | |
|---|---|---|
| ١١-إِنَّ ٱلَّذِينَ | *'Inna 'alladhīna* | Lo! those who |
| ءَامَنُوا۟ | *'āmanū* | believe |
| وَعَمِلُوا۟ ٱلصَّٰلِحَٰتِ | *wa-'amilu-(a)ṣ-ṣāliḥāti* | and do good deeds |
| لَهُمْ جَنَّٰتٌ | *la-hum jannāt(un)* | for them are Gardens |
| تَجْرِى | *tajrī* | flows |
| مِن تَحْتِهَا | *min taḥti-hā* | beneath which |
| ٱلْأَنْهَٰرُ | *'al-'anhāru* | the rivers |
| ذَٰلِكَ | *dhālika* | that is |
| ٱلْفَوْزُ ٱلْكَبِيرُ | *'al-fawzu-(a)l-kabīr(u)* | the great success |
| ١٢-إِنَّ بَطْشَ | *'Inna baṭsha* | Truly, the grip (punishment) |
| رَبِّكَ | *Rabbi-ka* | of your Lord |
| لَشَدِيدٌ | *la-shadīd(un)* | (is) very strong |

| | | |
|---|---|---|
| ١٣-إِنَّهُ هُوَ | *'Inna-hu Huwa* | Indeed! He is |
| يُبْدِئُ | *yubdi'u* | Who creates from the very beginning |
| وَيُعِيدُ | *wa-yu'īdu* | and (He) re-creates |
| ١٤-وَهُوَ ٱلْغَفُورُ | *Wa-Huwa-(a)l-Ghafūru* | And He is The Oft-Forgiving |
| ٱلْوَدُودُ | *'al-Wadūd(u)* | the Loving |
| ١٥-ذُو ٱلعَرْشِ ٱلْمَجِيدُ | *Dhu-(a)l-'Arshi-(a)l-Majīd(u)* | Lord of Throne, the Glorious |
| ١٦-فَعَّالٌ | *Fa''ālun* | The Doer |
| لِمَايُرِيدُ | *li-mā yurīd(u)* | of what He Wills |
| ١٧-هَلْ أَتَاكَ | *Hal 'atā-ka* | Has come to you ? |
| حَدِيثُ ٱلْجُنُودِ | *ḥadīthu-(a)l-junūd(i)* | the story of the forces |
| ١٨-فِرْعَوْنَ | *Fir'awna* | Of Pharaoh |
| وَثَمُودَ | *wa-Thamūd(a)* | and the people of *Thamūd* |
| ١٩-بَلِ ٱلَّذِينَ | *Bali-(a)lladhīna* | And yet those who |
| كَفَرُوا | *kafarū* | disbelieved |
| فِى تَكْذِيبٍ | *fī takdhīb(in)* | keep on rejecting, keep on denying |
| ٢٠-وَٱللَّهُ | *Wa-(A)llāhu* | But Allah |
| مِن وَرَآئِهِم | *min warā'i-him* | from behind them |
| مُّحِيطٌ | *muḥīṭ(un)* | surrounds |
| ٢١-بَلْ هُوَ | *Bal huwa* | Nay! this is, it is |
| قُرءَانٌ مَّجِيدٌ | *Qur'ānun Majīd(un)* | a Glorious Qur'ān. |
| ٢٢-فِي لَوحٍ | *Fī Lawḥin* | In a Tablet |
| مَحْفُوظٍ | *Maḥfūẓ(in)* | Guarded, Preserved |

**Lesson 12**

سُورَةُ الانْشِقَاق
آياتها ٢٥ — ترتيبها ٨٤

# *AL-'INSHIQĀQ, 84:1-15*

## THE RENDING ASUNDER / THE SUNDERING

**Revealed in Makkah**

---

**INTRODUCTION:**

This is one of the earlier Makkan *Suwar*. It deals with the prominent Makkan theme of the *'Ākhirah.* In subject matter, it is closely related to *Suwar* 81 and 82.

Rasūlullāh ﷺ said about these three *Suwar*: "Whoever wishes to see the Day of Judgment with his own eyes should read the *Suwar: Kuwwirat, Al-'Infiṭār and Al-'Inshiqāq."*

| **TRANSLITERATION:** | **ARABIC TEXT:** |
|---|---|
| *Bismillāhi-(a)r-Raḥmāni-(a)r-Raḥīm(i)* | بِسْمِ اللّٰهِ الرَّحْمٰنِ الرَّحِيْمِ |
| 1. *'Idha-(a)s-samā'un shaqqat* | إِذَا السَّمَآءُ انْشَقَّتْ ۝ |
| 2. *Wa 'adhinat li-Rabbi-hā wa ḥuqqat* | وَأَذِنَتْ لِرَبِّهَا وَحُقَّتْ ۝ |
| 3. *Wa 'idha-(a)l-'arḍu muddat* | وَإِذَا الْأَرْضُ مُدَّتْ ۝ |
| 4. *Wa 'alqat mā fī-hā wa takhallat* | وَأَلْقَتْ مَا فِيهَا وَتَخَلَّتْ ۝ |
| 5. *Wa 'adhinat li-Rabbi-hā wa ḥuqqat* | وَأَذِنَتْ لِرَبِّهَا وَحُقَّتْ ۝ |
| 6. *Yā 'ayyuha-(a)l-'insānu 'inna-ka kādiḥun* | يَٰٓأَيُّهَا الْإِنْسَانُ إِنَّكَ كَادِحٌ |
| *'ilā Rabbi-ka kadḥan fa-mulāqīh(i)* | إِلَىٰ رَبِّكَ كَدْحًا فَمُلَاقِيهِ ۝ |
| 7. *Fa-'ammā man 'ūtiya kitāba-hū bi-yamīnih(i)* | فَأَمَّا مَنْ أُوتِيَ كِتَٰبَهُۥ بِيَمِينِهِ ۝ |
| 8. *Fa-sawfa yuḥāsabu ḥisāban yasīrā(n)* | فَسَوْفَ يُحَاسَبُ حِسَابًا يَسِيرًا ۝ |
| 9. *Wa yanqalibu 'ilā 'ahli-hī masrūrā(n)* | وَيَنْقَلِبُ إِلَىٰٓ أَهْلِهِ مَسْرُورًا ۝ |

10. *Wa 'ammā man 'ūtiya kitāba-hu warā'a ẓahrihi* — وَأَمَّا مَنْ أُوتِيَ كِتَٰبَهُۥ وَرَآءَ ظَهْرِهِۦ ۝

11. *Fa-sawfa yad'ū thubūrā(n)* — فَسَوْفَ يَدْعُوا۟ ثُبُورًا ۝

12. *Wa yaṣlā sa'īrā(n)* — وَيَصْلَىٰ سَعِيرًا ۝

13. *'Inna-hū kāna fī 'ahli-hī masrūrā(n)* — إِنَّهُۥ كَانَ فِىٓ أَهْلِهِۦ مَسْرُورًا ۝

14. *'Inna-hū ẓanna 'an-lan yaḥūr(a)* — إِنَّهُۥ ظَنَّ أَن لَّن يَحُورَ ۝

15. *Balā 'inna Rabba-hū kāna bi-hī baṣīrā(n)* — بَلَىٰٓ إِنَّ رَبَّهُۥ كَانَ بِهِۦ بَصِيرًا ۝

**TRANSLATIONS**:

In the name of Allāh, Most Gracious,
Most Merciful.

1. When the Sky is rent asunder,
2. And listens to (the Command of) its Lord,
and it must need (do so)
3. And when the Earth is flattened out,
4. And casts forth what is within it.
And becomes (clean) empty,
5. And listens to (the command of) its Lord,
and it must need (do so);
(then will come home the full Reality).
6. O you man! Truly you are ever toiling on
toward your Lord painfully toiling,
but you shall meet Him.
7. Then he who is given his
record in his right hand,
8. Soon will his account be taken
by an easy reckoning,
9. And he will turn to his people, rejoicing!
10. But he who is given his
Record behind his back,
11. Soon will he cry for Perdition,

In the name of Allāh, the Beneficent,
the Merciful.

1. When the heaven is split asunder
2. And attentive to her Lord
in fear,
3. And when the earth is spread out
4. And has cast out all that was in her,
and is empty
5. And attentive to her Lord
in fear!
6. You, verily, O' man, are working
toward your Lord a work which you will
meet (in His presence).
7. Then whoso is given his
account in his right hand
8. He truly will receive
an easy reckoning
9. And will return to his folk in joy.
10. But whoso is given his
account behind his back,
11. He surely will invoke destruction

12. And he will enter a Blazing Fire.
13. Truly, did he go about among his people, rejoicing!
14. Truly, did he think that he would not have to return (to Us)
15. No, No! for his Lord was (ever) watchful of him!

12. And be thrown to scorching fire.
13. He verily lived joyous with his folk,
14. He verily deemed that he would never return (to Allāh).
15. Nay, but lo! his Lord is ever looking on him!

---

**EXPLANATION:**

84:1-5. These verses, like those in *Suwar* 81 and 82, describe the signs of the *Qiyāmah*: the sky will split and the Earth will flatten and overthrow whatever it had contained. The entire cosmic order, which runs its course according to certain rules pre-determined by Allāh سبحانه وتعالى, will obey His new Command and turn upside down.

84:6. All human beings follow a path that leads to Allāh سبحانه وتعالى. No one can escape death or the Day of Judgment.

84:7-9. The righteous will receive their Book of Deeds in their right hands and will return to their family and friends, joyous in their success.

84:10-15. The wicked will receive their Book of Deeds in their left hands and enter the Fire in gloom. Such people led lives of pride and pleasure and were unconcerned with the Hereafter. On that Day, they will suffer the consequences of their actions.

**WE HAVE LEARNED:**

* Every human being, a Believer and a non-believer alike, are moving toward their Lord.
* On the Day of Judgment the Righteous will be given their book of deeds in their right hands.
* The wicked will be given their books of deeds in their left hands.

## VOCABULARY

## ٨٤-سُورَةُ ٱلْانْشِقَاق

| | | |
|---|---|---|
| ١-إِذَا ٱلسَّمَآءُ | *'Idha-(a)s-samā'u* | When the sky, heaven |
| انْشَقَّتْ | *'inshaqqat* | is split asunder |
| ٢-وَأَذِنَتْ | *Wa-'adhinat* | And listens, and hearkens |
| لِرَبِّهَا | *li-Rabbi-hā* | to its Lord |
| وَحُقَّتْ | *wa-ḥuqqat* | in duty bound, in fear |
| ٣-وَإِذَا ٱلْأَرْضُ | *Wa-'idha-(a)l-'arḍu* | And when the Earth is |
| مُدَّتْ | *muddat* | flattened out, spread out |
| ٤-وَأَلْقَتْ | *Wa-'alqat* | And casts forth, has cast out |
| مَا فِيهَا | *mā fī-hā* | what is within it |
| وَتَخَلَّتْ | *wa-takhallat* | and is empty |
| ٥-وَأَذِنَتْ | *Wa-'adhinat* | And listens, and hearkens |
| لِرَبِّهَا | *li-Rabbi-hā* | to her Lord |
| وَحُقَّتْ | *wa-ḥuqqat* | in duty bound, in fear |
| ٦-يَـٰٓأَيُّهَا ٱلْإِنسَـٰنُ | *Yā-'ayyuha-(a)l-insānu* | O you man, O you humankind |
| إِنَّكَ كَادِحٌ | *'inna-ka kādiḥ(un)* | indeed! you are toiling on, working on |
| إِلَىٰ رَبِّكَ | *'ilā Rabbi-ka* | toward Your Lord |
| كَدْحًا | *kadḥa(n)* | painfully toiling, a hard work |
| فَمُلَـٰقِيهِ | *fa-mulāqīh(i)* | but you shall meet him |
| ٧-فَأَمَّا مَنْ | *Fa-'ammā man* | then, he who |
| أُوتِىَ | *'ūtiya* | is given |
| كِتَـٰبَهُۥ | *kitāba-hū* | his record , his book (of accounts) |

| | | |
|---|---|---|
| بِيَمِينِهِ | *bi-yamīni-hi* | in his right-hand |
| ٨-فَسَوْفَ يُحَاسَبُ | *Fa-sawfa yuḥāsabu* | soon his account will be taken |
| حِسَاباً يَسِيراً | *ḥisāban yasīra(n)* | by an easy accounting |
| ٩-وَيَنقَلِبُ | *Wa-yanqalibu* | And he will return |
| إِلَىٰ أَهْلِهِ | *'ilā 'ahli-hī* | to his people, to his folk |
| مَسْرُوراً | *masrūra(n)* | rejoicing joyfully |
| ١٠-وَأَمَّا مَنْ | *Wa-'ammā man* | But he who |
| أُوتِيَ كِتَـٰبَهُ | *'ūtiya kitāba-hū* | is given his book |
| وَرَآءَ ظَهْرِهِ | *warā'a ẓahri-h(i)* | behind his back |
| ١١-فَسَوفَ يَدْعُواْ | *Fa-sawfa yad'ū* | soon he will cry |
| ثُبُوراً | *t͟hubūrā(n)* | for perdition, for destruction |
| ١٢-وَيَصْلَىٰ | *Wa-yuṣlā* | And he will be exposed to the blaze of |
| سَعِيراً | *sa'īrā(n)* | scorching fire |
| ١٣-إِنَّهُ كَانَ | *'Inna-hū kāna* | He indeed lived (was) |
| فِيٓ أَهْلِهِ | *fī 'ahli-hī* | among his people, |
| مَسْرُوراً | *masrūrā(n)* | rejoicing, happily |
| ١٤-إِنَّهُ ظَنَّ | *'Inna-hu ẓanna* | He, did truly, think |
| أَن لَّن يَّحُورَ | *'an lan yaḥūr(a)* | that he would never return |
| ١٥-بَلَىٰٓ إِنَّ | *Balā 'inna* | Nay, but indeed |
| رَبَّهُ | *Rabba-hu* | his Lord |
| كَانَ بِهِ بَصِيراً | *kāna bi-hī baṣīrā(n)* | was on him watchful |

*Lesson 13*

# *AL-INSHIQĀQ, 84:16-25*

## THE RENDING ASUNDER / THE SUNDERING

**Revealed in Makkah**

| **TRANSLITERATION**: | **ARABIC TEXT**: |
|---|---|
| 16. *Fa-lā 'uqsimu bi-(a)sh-shafaq(i)* | فَلَآ أُقْسِمُ بِالشَّفَقِ ○- |
| 17. *Wa-(a)l-laili wa mā wasaq(a)* | وَالَّيْلِ وَمَا وَسَقَ ○- |
| 18. *Wal qamari 'idha-(a)t-tasaq(a)* | وَالْقَمَرِ إِذَا اتَّسَقَ ○- |
| 19. *La-tarkabunna ṭabaqan 'an ṭabaq(in)* | لَتَرْكَبُنَّ طَبَقًا عَنْ طَبَقٍ ○- |
| 20. *Fa-mā la-hum lā-yu'minūn(a)* | فَمَا لَهُمْ لَا يُؤْمِنُونَ ○- |
| 21. *Wa 'idha quri'a 'alai-himu-(a)l-Qur'ānu lā yasjudūn(a)* | وَإِذَا قُرِئَ عَلَيْهِمُ الْقُرْءَانُ لَا يَسْجُدُونَ ○- |
| 22. *Bali-(a)lladhīna kafarū yukadhdhibūn(a)* | بَلِ الَّذِينَ كَفَرُوا يُكَذِّبُونَ ○- |
| 23. *Wa-(A)llāhu 'a'lamu bi-mā yū'ūn(a)* | وَاللَّهُ أَعْلَمُ بِمَا يُوعُونَ ○- |
| 24. *Fa-bashshir-hum bi 'adhābin 'alīm(in)* | فَبَشِّرْهُمْ بِعَذَابٍ أَلِيمٍ ○- |
| 25. *'Illa-(a)lladhīna 'āmanū wa 'amilu-(a)ṣ-ṣāliḥāti* | إِلَّا الَّذِينَ ءَامَنُوا وَعَمِلُوا الصَّٰلِحَٰتِ- |
| *la-hum 'ajrun ghairu mamnūn(in)* | لَهُمْ أَجْرٌ غَيْرُ مَمْنُونٍ ○ |

**TRANSLATIONS**:

16. So I do call to witness the ruddy glow of Sunset;
17. The night and its Homing;
18. And the Moon in her Fullness;
19. You shall surely travel

16. Oh, I swear by the afterglow of sunset,
17. And by the night and all that it enshrouds,
18. And by the moon when she is at the full,
19. That you shall journey on

from stage to stage.
20. What then is the matter with them, that they believe not?
21. And when the Qur'ān is read to them, they fall not prostrate,
22. But on the contrary the Unbelievers reject (it)
23. But Allāh has full Knowledge of what they secrete (in their breasts)
24. So announce to them a Penalty Grievous,
25. Except to those who believe and work righteous deeds: for them is a reward that will never fail.

from plane to plane
20. What ailes them, then, that they believe not
21. And, when the Qur'ān is recited to them, worship not (Allāh)?
22. Nay, but those who disbelieve will deny;
23. And Allāh Knows best what they are hiding.
24. So give them tidings of a painful doom,
25. Save those who believe and do good works, for theirs is a reward unfailing.

---

## EXPLANATION:

84:16-19. Here three creations of Allāh سبحانه وتعالى : the glow of sunset, the night and the moon, are mentioned as witnesses to the impermanence of this life. The fact remains that human beings are constantly moving from one stage to another. This applies to the life of this world as well as to that of the Hereafter.

84:20-24. For a thinking individual, there are all the signs to believe in Allāh سبحانه وتعالى and the Day of Judgment, however, the *Kuffār* persist in their disbelief. They do not prostrate to Allāh سبحانه وتعالى when they hear His Message in the Qur'ān. Instead they deny the Truth. The unbelievers are issued a warning of a grievous punishment for their disobedience.

84:25. Those who believe and do righteous deeds will receive generous reward from their Lord; and Allāh سبحانه وتعالى never fails in His promise.

## WE HAVE LEARNED:

* Every human being is moving from one stage to another stage to meet his Lord.
* The *Kuffār* do not believe and do not heed to the message of the Qur'ān.
* They deny the Qur'ān and the *'Ākhirah*; for their denial they shall be held accountable.

### VOCABULARY

٨٤-سُورَةُ ٱلْأَنْشِقَاق

| | | |
|---|---|---|
| ١٦-فَلَآ أُقْسِمُ | *Fa-lā 'uqsimu* | So, I do call to witness |
| بِٱلشَّفَقِ | *bi-(a)sh-shafaqi* | the ruddy glow of sunset |

| | | |
|---|---|---|
| ١٧-وَٱلَّيْلِ | *Wa-(a)l-laili* | by the night |
| وَمَا وَسَقَ | *wa-mā wasaqa* | and that it enshrouds |
| ١٨-وَٱلْقَمَرِ | *Wa-(a)l-qamari* | By the moon |
| إِذَا ٱتَّسَقَ | *'idha-(a)t-tasaqa* | when she is full |
| ١٩-لَتَرْكَبُنَّ | *la-tarkabunna* | Surely! you shall travel |
| طَبَقًاعَنْ طَبَقٍ | *ṭabaqan 'an ṭabaq(in)* | from stage to stage |
| ٢٠-فَمَا لَهُمْ | *Fa-mā la-hum* | What is the matter with them |
| لَا يُؤْمِنُونَ | *lā yu'minūn(a)* | they believe not |
| ٢١-وَإِذَا قُرِئَ | *Wa-'idhā quri'a* | And when is read |
| عَلَيْهِمُ ٱلْقُرْءَانُ | *'alai-himu-(a)l-Qur'ānu* | to them the Qur'ān |
| لَا يَسْجُدُونَ | *lā yasjudūn(a)* | fall not prostrate, do not prostrate |
| ٢٢-بَلِ ٱلَّذِينَ | *Bali-(a)lladhīna* | But those who |
| كَفَرُوا | *kafarū* | disbelieve, do *kufr* |
| يُكَذِّبُونَ | *yukadhdhibūn(a)* | they reject, deny |
| ٢٣-وَٱللَّهُ أَعْلَمُ | *Wa-(A)llāhu 'a'lamu* | But, Allah has Full Knowledge |
| بِمَا يُوعُونَ | *bi-mā yū'ūn(a)* | of what they hide |
| ٢٤-فَبَشِّرْهُم | *Fa-bashshir-hum* | So announce to them |
| بِعَذَابٍ أَلِيمٍ | *bi-'adhābin 'alīm(in)* | of a grievous penalty, of a painful doom |
| ٢٥-إِلَّا ٱلَّذِينَ | *'Illa-(a)lladhīna* | Except to those |
| ءَامَنُوا | *'āmanū* | who believe |
| وَعَمِلُوا ٱلصَّٰلِحَٰتِ | *wa-'amilu-(a)ṣ-ṣāliḥāti* | and do righteous deeds, do good |
| لَهُمْ أَجْرٌ | *la-hum 'ajrun* | for them is a Reward |
| غَيْرُ مَمْنُونٍ | *ghairu mamnūn(i)* | that will never fail, unfailing |

**Lesson 14**

سُورَةُ المُطَفِّفِين — آياتها ٣٦ — ترتيبها ٨٣

# AL-MUṬAFFIFĪN, 83:1-17

## THE DEALERS IN FRAUD / DEFRAUDING

**Revealed in Makkah**

---

**INTRODUCTION:**

This is one of the earliest Makkan *Suwar*. In subject matter, it is closely related to *Sūrah* 81 and *Sūrah* 82. It describes the cataclysmic events that will take place before the Day of Judgment. A new era will dawn, in which both good and evil will be judged.

| **TRANSLITERATION:** | **ARABIC TEXT:** |
|---|---|
| *Bismillāhi-(a)r-Raḥmāni-(a)r-Raḥīm(i)* | بِسْمِ اللَّهِ الرَّحْمَٰنِ الرَّحِيمِ |
| 1. *Wailun li-(a)l-muṭaffifīn(a)* | وَيْلٌ لِّلْمُطَفِّفِينَ ۝ |
| 2. *'Alladhīna 'idha-(a)ktālū 'al-an-nāsi yastawfūn(a)* | الَّذِينَ إِذَا اكْتَالُوا عَلَى النَّاسِ يَسْتَوْفُونَ ۝ |
| 3. *Wa 'idhā kālū-hum 'aw-wazanū-hum yukhsirūn(a)* | وَإِذَا كَالُوهُمْ أَو وَّزَنُوهُمْ يُخْسِرُونَ ۝ |
| 4. *'Alā yaẓunnu 'ūlā'ika 'anna-hum mab'ūthūn(a)* | أَلَا يَظُنُّ أُولَٰئِكَ أَنَّهُم مَّبْعُوثُونَ ۝ |
| 5. *Lī-yawmin 'aẓīm(in)* | لِيَوْمٍ عَظِيمٍ ۝ |
| 6. *Yawma yaqūmu-(a)n-nāsu li-Rabbi-(a)l-'ālamīn(a)* | يَوْمَ يَقُومُ النَّاسُ لِرَبِّ الْعَالَمِينَ ۝ |
| 7. *Kallā 'inna kitāba-(a)l-fujjāri la-fī sijjīn(in)* | كَلَّا إِنَّ كِتَابَ الْفُجَّارِ لَفِي سِجِّينٍ ۝ |
| 8. *Wa mā 'adrā-ka mā sijjīn(un)* | وَمَا أَدْرَاكَ مَا سِجِّينٌ ۝ |
| 9. *Kitābun marqūm(un)* | كِتَابٌ مَّرْقُومٌ ۝ |
| 10. *Wailun yawma'idhin li(a)l-mukadhdhibīn(a)* | وَيْلٌ يَوْمَئِذٍ لِّلْمُكَذِّبِينَ ۝ |
| 11. *'Alladhīna yukadhdhibūna bi-yawmi-(a)d-dīn(i)* | الَّذِينَ يُكَذِّبُونَ بِيَوْمِ الدِّينِ ۝ |

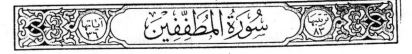

12. *Wa mā yukadhdhibu bi-hī 'illā kullu mu'tadin 'athīm(in)* — وَمَا يُكَذِّبُ بِهِۦٓ إِلَّا كُلُّ مُعْتَدٍ أَثِيمٍ ۝

13. *'Idhā tutlā 'alaihi 'āyātunā qāla 'asāṭīru-(a)l-'awwalīn(a)* — إِذَا تُتْلَىٰ عَلَيْهِ ءَايَٰتُنَا قَالَ أَسَٰطِيرُ ٱلْأَوَّلِينَ ۝

14. *Kallā bal rāna 'alā qulūbi-him mā kānū yaksibūn(a)* — كَلَّا بَلْ رَانَ عَلَىٰ قُلُوبِهِم مَّا كَانُوا۟ يَكْسِبُونَ ۝

15. *Kallā 'inna-hum 'an Rabbi-him* — كَلَّآ إِنَّهُمْ عَن رَّبِّهِمْ

*yawma'idhin la-maḥjūbūn(a)* — يَوْمَئِذٍ لَّمَحْجُوبُونَ ۝

16. *Thumma 'inna-hum la-ṣālū-(a)l-jaḥīm(i)* — ثُمَّ إِنَّهُمْ لَصَالُوا۟ ٱلْجَحِيمِ ۝

17. *Thumma yuqālu hādha-(a)lladhī* — ثُمَّ يُقَالُ هَٰذَا ٱلَّذِى

*kuntum bi-hī tukadhdhibūn(a)* — كُنتُم بِهِۦ تُكَذِّبُونَ ۝

**TRANSLATIONS:**

In the name of Allāh, Most Gracious, Most Merciful.

1. Woe to those that deal in fraud,
2. Those who, when they have to receive by measure from men, exact full measure,
3. But when they have to give by measure or weight to men, give less than due.
4. Do they not think that they will be called to account?
5. On a Mighty Day,
6. A Day when (all) mankind will stand before the Lord of the Worlds?
7. No! Surely the Record of the Wicked is (preserved) in *Sijjīn*.
8. And what will explain to you what *Sijjīn* is?
9. (There is) a Register (fully) inscribed.
10. Woe, that Day, to those that deny
11. Those that deny the Day of Judgment.
12. And none can deny it but the Transgressor beyond bounds, the Sinner!

In the name of Allāh, the Beneficent, the Merciful.

1. Woe to the defrauders:
2. Those who when they take the measure from mankind demand it full,
3. But if they measure to them or weigh for them, they cause them loss.
4. Do such (men) not consider that they will be raised again
5. To an awful Day:
6. The day when (all) mankind will stand before the Lord of the Worlds?
7. Nay, but the record of the vile is in *Sijjīn*.
8. Ah! what will convey to you what *Sijjīn* is!
9. A written record.
10. Woe to the repudiators on that day!
11. Those who deny the Day of Judgment
12. Which none deny save each criminal transgressor,

13. When Our Signs are rehearsed to him, he says,
    "Tales of Ancients!"
14. By no means! But on their hearts is the stain of the (ill) which they do!
15. Truly, from (the Light of) their Lord, that Day, will they be veiled.
16. Further, they will enter The Fire of Hell.
17. Further, it will be said to them: "This is the (reality) which you rejected as false!"

13. Who, when you read to him Our Revelations, say:
    (Mere) fables of the men of old.
14. Nay, but that which they have earned is rust upon their hearts.
15. Nay, but surely on that day they will be covered from (the mercy of) their Lord.
16. Then lo! they verily will burn in hell,
17. And it will be said (to them): This is that which you used to deny.

---

## EXPLANATION:

83:1-3. The fraudulent are the people who deal in fraud. These people are strongly condemned in this *Sūrah*. The fraud is to deceive others of their rights. An example of fraud is offered in verses 2 and 3. The fraudulent are unjust and unfair in their dealings; when they take they want to receive more than their due share and when they give, they give less than other people's due. In their commercial, as well as, social dealings these people are stingy, unfair and unjust.

83:4-6. The reason for this immoral behavior of the fraudulent people is their disbelief in the 'Ākhirah, when everyone will be presented before Allāh ﷻ for judgment.

83:7-11. On the Day of Judgment everyone will be presented before Allāh ﷻ with their record of deeds. The record of deeds of the Wicked are kept in a register which is called the *Sijjīn*. The *Sijjīn* is derived from the Arabic root *Sajana* meaning to send someone to jail. These books of records, the *Sijjīn*, will be used to send the Wicked to the dungeons of punishment.

83:12-13. The reality of the 'Ākhirah is denied by the disbelievers because they do not want to accept the responsibility of their evil actions in this world. These people do not believe the Revelation when it informs them of the history of earlier people who were condemned for their evil deeds or blessed for their good deeds by Allāh ﷻ . When they hear these stories they laugh and make fun of the words of Allāh ﷻ .

83:14-17. Allāh has created everyone on the *Fiṭrah,* the true innocent nature. The good deeds continue to keep our hearts clean and shining and evil deeds make it dusty and rusted. If the evil-doers do not repent and ask the forgiveness of Allāh their hearts are totally blocked from seeing the Truth. In the *'Ākhirah* they will not be able to experience the Glory of Allāh and the joy of the *Jannah.* For their denial of the Truth these liars and defrauders will be thrown into Hell.

**WE HAVE LEARNED:**

* The people who do fraud will be punished for their crimes.
* These dishonest people deny the Day of Judgment.
* The evil acts of the Wicked are being written in a book called *Sijjīn.*

## VOCABULARY

### ٨٣-سُورَةُ ٱلْمُطَفِّفِينَ

| | | |
|---|---|---|
| ١-وَيْلٌ لِّلْمُطَفِّفِينَ | *Wailun li-(a)l-muṭaffifīn(a)* | Woe to defrauders |
| ٢-ٱلَّذِينَ | *'Alladhīna* | Those who |
| إِذَا ٱكْتَالُوا | *'idha-(a)ktālū* | when they take by measure |
| عَلَى ٱلنَّاسِ | *'ala-(a)n-nās(i)* | from people |
| يَسْتَوْفُونَ | *yastawfūn(a)* | demand fully, take full measure |
| ٣-وَإِذَا كَالُوهُمْ | *Wa-'idhā kālū-hum* | And when they give by measure |
| أَو وَّزَنُوهُم | *'aw wazanū-hum* | or weigh to them |
| يُخْسِرُونَ | *yukhsirūn(a)* | they cause them loss, give less than due |
| ٤-أَلَا يَظُنُّ | *'Alā yaẓunnu* | Do (they) not think, consider |
| أُولَـٰئِكَ | *'ulā'ika* | they |
| أَنَّهُم مَّبْعُوثُونَ | *'anna-hum mab'ūthūna* | truly they will be raised again |
| ٥-لِيَوْمٍ عَظِيمٍ | *li-yawmin 'aẓīm(in)* | on a Mighty Day |

| | | |
|---|---|---|
| ٦-يَوْمَ | *Yawma* | A Day |
| يَقُومُ | *yaqūmu* | when stands |
| ٱلنَّاسُ | *'an-nās(u)* | all humankind |
| لِرَبِّ ٱلْعَـٰلَمِينَ | *li-Rabbi-(a)l-'Ālamīn(a)* | before the Lord of the Worlds |
| ٧-كَلَّآ إِنَّ | *Kallā 'inna* | Nay, surely |
| كِتَـٰبَ ٱلْفُجَّارِ | *kitāba-(a)l-fujjār(i)* | the record of the wicked persons |
| لَفِى سِجِّينٍ | *la-fī sijjīn(in)* | is in *sijjīn* |
| ٨-وَمَآ أَدْرَىٰكَ | *Wa-mā 'adrā-ka* | And what explain to you |
| مَا سِجِّينٌ | *mā sijjīn(un)* | what *sijjīn* is |
| ٩-كِتَـٰبٌ مَّرْقُومٌ | *Kitābun marqūm(un)* | Written record, registered book |
| ١٠-وَيْلٌ يَوْمَئِذٍ | *Wailun yawma'idhin* | woe, on that Day |
| لِّلْمُكَذِّبِينَ | *li-(a)l-mukadhdhibīn(a)* | on those who deny, unto the repudiators |
| ١١-ٱلَّذِينَ يُكَذِّبُونَ | *'alladhina yukadhdhibūna* | those who deny |
| بِيَوْمِ ٱلدِّينِ | *bi-Yawmi-(a)d-Dīn(i)* | to the Day of Judgment |
| ١٢- وَمَا يُكَذِّبُ | *Wa-mā yukadhdhibu* | And none can deny |
| بِهِۦٓ | *bi-hī* | to it |
| إِلَّا كُلُّ | *'illā kullu* | except every |
| مُعْتَدٍ | *mu'tadin* | criminal, transgressor |
| أَثِيمٍ | *'athīm(in)* | sinner |
| ١٣-إِذَا تُتْلَىٰ | *'Idhā tutlā* | When rehearsed, when read |
| عَلَيْهِ ءَايَـٰتُنَا | *'alai-hi 'āyātu-nā* | unto him Our Signs, Our Revelations |

| | | |
|---|---|---|
| قَالَ | *qāla* | he says |
| أَسَٰطِيرُ | *'asāṭir(u)* | tales, fables |
| ٱلأَوَّلِينَ | *'al-'awwalīn(a)* | men of old, of ancients |
| ١٤-كَلَّاۖ بَلْۜ رَانَ | *Kallā bal rāna* | By no means, the rust, the stain |
| عَلَىٰ قُلُوبِهِمْ | *'alā qulūbi-him* | on their hearts |
| مَّا كَانُوا يَكْسِبُونَ | *mā kānū yaksibūn(a)* | which they do, which they have earned |
| ١٥-كَلَّاۤ إِنَّهُمْ | *Kallā 'inna-hum* | Verily, Indeed they |
| عَن رَّبِّهِمْ | *'an Rabbi-him* | from their Lord |
| يَوْمَئِذ | *yawma'idhin* | that Day |
| لَّمَحْجُوبُونَ | *la-maḥjūbūn(a)* | they will be veiled |
| ١٦-ثُمَّ إِنَّهُمْ | *Thuma 'inna-hum* | Then surely, they |
| لَصَالُوا | *la-ṣālū* | (they) will enter, will burn in |
| ٱلْجَحِيمِ | *'al-Jaḥīm(i)* | the fire of Hell |
| ١٧-ثُمَّ يُقَالُ | *Thuma yuqālu* | Then, further it will be said |
| هَٰذَا ٱلَّذِى | *hādha-(a)lladhī* | this is the reality |
| كُنْتُم بِهِ | *kuntum bi-hī* | to which |
| تُكَذِّبُونَ | *tukadhdhibūn(a)* | you denied, rejected as false |

*Lesson 15*

# *AL-MUṬAFFIFĪN, 83:18-36*

## THE DEALERS IN FRAUD / DEFRAUDING

**Revealed in Makkah**

---

| **TRANSLITERATION**: | **ARABIC TEXT**: |
|---|---|
| 18. *Kallā 'inna kitāba-(a)l-'abrāri la-fī 'illiyyīn(a)* | -كَلَّآ إِنَّ كِتَٰبَ ٱلْأَبْرَارِ لَفِى عِلِّيِّينَ ○ |
| 19. *Wa mā 'adrā-ka mā 'illiyyūn(a)* | -وَمَآ أَدْرَىٰكَ مَا عِلِّيُّونَ ○ |
| 20. *Kitābun marqūm(un)* | -كِتَٰبٌ مَّرْقُومٌ ○ |
| 21. *Yashhadu-hu-(a)l-muqarrabūn(a)* | -يَشْهَدُهُ ٱلْمُقَرَّبُونَ ○ |
| 22. *'Inna-(a)l-'abrāra lafī na'īm(in)* | -إِنَّ ٱلْأَبْرَارَ لَفِى نَعِيمٍ ○ |
| 23. *'Ala-(a)l-'arā'iki yanẓurūn(a)* | -عَلَى ٱلْأَرَآئِكِ يَنظُرُونَ ○ |
| 24. *Ta'rifu fī wujūhi-him naḍrata-(a)n-na'īm(i)* | -تَعْرِفُ فِى وُجُوهِهِمْ نَضْرَةَ ٱلنَّعِيمِ ○ |
| 25. *Yusqawna min raḥīqin makhtūm(in)* | -يُسْقَوْنَ مِن رَّحِيقٍ مَّخْتُومٍ ○ |
| 26. *Khitāmu-hū miskun wa fī dhālika* | -خِتَٰمُهُۥ مِسْكٌ ۚ وَفِى ذَٰلِكَ |
| *fa-l-yatanāfasi-(a)l-mutanāfisūn(a)* | فَلْيَتَنَافَسِ ٱلْمُتَنَٰفِسُونَ ○ |
| 27. *Wa mizāju-hu min Tasnīm(in)* | -وَمِزَاجُهُۥ مِن تَسْنِيمٍ ○ |
| 28. *'Ainan yashrabu bi-ha-(a)l-muqarrabūn(a)* | -عَيْنًا يَشْرَبُ بِهَا ٱلْمُقَرَّبُونَ ○ |
| 29. *'Inna-(a)lladhīna 'ajramū kānū* | -إِنَّ ٱلَّذِينَ أَجْرَمُوا۟ كَانُوا۟ |
| *mina-(a)lladhīna 'āmanū yaḍḥakūn(a)* | مِنَ ٱلَّذِينَ ءَامَنُوا۟ يَضْحَكُونَ ○ |
| 30. *Wa 'idhā marrū bi-him yataghāmazūn(a)* | -وَإِذَا مَرُّوا۟ بِهِمْ يَتَغَامَزُونَ ○ |
| 31. *Wa 'idha-(a)n-qalabū 'ilā 'ahli-himu-(a)n-qalabū fakihīn(a)* | -وَإِذَا ٱنقَلَبُوٓا۟ إِلَىٰٓ أَهْلِهِمُ ٱنقَلَبُوا۟ فَكِهِينَ ○ |

32. *Wa 'idhā ra'aw-hum qālū 'inna hā'ulā'i laḍāllūn(a)* وَإِذَا رَأَوْهُمْ قَالُوٓا إِنَّ هَٰٓؤُلَآءِ لَضَآلُّونَ ۝

33. *Wa mā 'ursilū 'alai-him ḥāfiẓīn(a)* وَمَآ أُرْسِلُوا عَلَيْهِمْ حَٰفِظِينَ ۝

34. *Fa-(a)l-yawma-(a)lladhīna 'āmanū* فَٱلْيَوْمَ ٱلَّذِينَ ءَامَنُوا

*mina-(a)l-kuffāri yaḍḥakūn(a)* مِنَ ٱلْكُفَّارِ يَضْحَكُونَ ۝

35. *'Ala-(a)l-'arā'iki yanẓurūn(a)* عَلَى ٱلْأَرَآئِكِ يَنظُرُونَ ۝

36. *Hal thuwwiba-(a)l-kuffāru mā kānū yaf'alūn(a)* هَلْ ثُوِّبَ ٱلْكُفَّارُ مَا كَانُوا يَفْعَلُونَ ۝

**TRANSLATIONS:**

18. No, truly the Record of the Righteous is (preserved) in *'Illiyīn*.
19. And what will explain to you what *'Illiyūn* is?
20. There is a Register (fully) inscribed,
21. To which bear witness those Nearest (to Allāh).
22. Truly the Righteous will be in Bliss:
23. On Thrones (of Dignity) will they command a sight (of all things).
24. You will recognize in their faces the beaming brightness of Bliss.
25. Their thirst will be slaked with Pure Wine sealed:
26. The seal of it will be musk; and for this let those aspire, who have aspirations:
27. With it will be (given) a mixture of *Tasnīm*
28. A spring, from (the waters) of which drink those Nearest to Allāh.
29. Those in sin used to laugh at those who believed,
30. And whenever they passed by them, used to wink at each other (in mockery);
31. And when they returned to their own people, they would return jesting;

18. Nay, but the record of the righteous is in *'Illiyīn*.
19. Ah, what will convey to you what *'Iliyūn* is!
20. A written record.
21. Attested by those who are brought near (to their Lord).
22. Lo! the righteous verily are in delight,
23. On couches, gazing,
24. You wilt know in their faces the radiance of delight.
25. They are given to drink of a a pure wine, sealed,
26. Whose seal is musk -- For this let (all) those strive who strive for bliss.
27. And mixed with water of *Tasnīm*,
28. A spring whence those brought near to Allāh drink.
29. Lo! the guilty used to laugh at those who believed,
30. And wink one to another when they passed them;
31. And when they returned to their own folk they returned jesting:

| | |
|---|---|
| 32. And whenever they saw them, they would say, "Look! these are the people truly astray!" | 32. And when they saw them they said: Lo! these have gone astray. |
| 33. But they had not been sent as keepers over them! | 33. Yet they were not sent as guardians over them. |
| 34. But on this Day the Believers will laugh at the Unbelievers: | 34. This day it is those who believe who have the laugh of disbelievers, |
| 35. On Thrones (of Dignity) they will command (a sight) (of all things). | 35. On high couches, gazing. |
| 36. Will not Unbelievers have been paid back for what they did? | 36. Are not the disbelievers paid for what they used to do? |

---

**EXPLANATION**:

83:18-21. In contrast to the Wicked will be the situation of the Righteous. Their records of good deeds will be in a separate register called the *'Illiyyīn*. The *'Illiyyīn* is derived from the Arabic root *'alawa*, meaning to raise someone high or to honor someone. These registers will be like the roll of honors in this world for the achievers. These books of records, the *'Illiyyīn*, will be a source of pleasure and a witness for the *'Illiyyūn*, the honored and Righteous owners of *Jannah*.

83:22-25. The *'Illiyyūn*, the Honored Righteous will enjoy the pleasures of the *'Ākhirah*. Seated on the high thrones of dignity, their faces will glow with light of their good deeds. They will be offered the pure wines of the *Jannah*. These wines of *Jannah* will not make people drunk but will give them special pleasures. No words can describe their taste.

83:26-28. Here are two beautiful descriptions of the wine of the *Jannah* that the Righteous must aspire to drink. It will be sealed with the seal of musk, that is its purity will be ensured. It will be mixed with the *Tasnīm*, the water of heavenly fountain. Musk represents a fragrance and *Tasnīm* literally means the fullness, height and glory. Its water is offered to those who are closest to Allāh سبحانه وتعالى and most honored in His Sight. We should understand that these are worldly descriptions of a reality that is beyond our present level of understanding. We can aspire for it and strive to achieve it.

83:29-33. On the Day of Judgment the reality of the *'Ākhirah* will be visible to all. In this world the Wicked could make fun and laugh at the Righteous. They could pass sarcastic and insulting remarks as they pass by the Righteous. The Wicked behaved as if they were acting against the Righteous with full authority. Allāh سبحانه وتعالى had granted no such authority to them.

83:34-36. On the Day of Judgment the Believers will have the last laugh as they would sit on their couches enjoying the fruits of their good deeds laughing at the stupidity of the *Kuffār* who had missed their opportunity.

**WE HAVE LEARNED**:

* The records of the Righteous will be written in the books called *'Illiyūn.*
* The Righteous will enjoy the pleasures of *Jannah.*
* The Believers were laughed at by the *Kuffār* in this world, then it will be their turn to laugh at them.

## VOCABULARY

### ٨٣-سُورَةُ ٱلْمُطَفِّفِينَ

| | | |
|---|---|---|
| ١٨-كَلاَّ إِنَّ | *Kallā 'inna* | By no means, but |
| كِتَٰبَ ٱلْأَبْرَارِ | *kitāba-(a)l-'abrāri* | the record of the righteous |
| لَفِى عِلِّيِّينَ | *la-fī 'illiyyīn(a)* | indeed is in the *'illiyin*, surely is in highest places |
| ١٩-وَمَآ أَدْرَىٰكَ | *Wa-mā 'adrā-ka* | And what will explain to you |
| مَا عِلِّيُّونَ | *ma 'illiyyūn(a)* | what *'illiyun* is, what the highest places are |
| ٢٠-كِتَٰبٌ مَّرْقُومٌ | *kitābun marqūm(un)* | a written register, a written record |
| ٢١-يَشْهَدُهُ | *Yashhadu-hu* | Attested by |
| ٱلْمُقَرَّبُونَ | *'al-muqarrabūn(a)* | the nearest, who are brought near ( to Allah) |
| ٢٢-إِنَّ ٱلْأَبْرَارَ | *'Inna-(a)l-'abrāra* | Indeed, the righteous |
| لَفِى نَعِيمٍ | *la-fī na'īm(in)* | will be in bliss |
| ٢٣-عَلَى ٱلْأَرَآئِكِ | *'Ala-(a)l-'arā'iki* | On the couches |
| يَنظُرُونَ | *yanẓurūn(a)* | gazing, looking |
| ٢٤-تَعْرِفُ | *Ta'rifu* | you will know, you will recognise |
| فِى وُجُوهِهِمْ | *fī wujūhi-him* | in their faces |
| نَضْرَةَ ٱلنَّعِيمِ | *naḍrata-(a)n-na'īm(i)* | radiance of bliss, brightness of delight |

| | | |
|---|---|---|
| ٢٥-يُسْقَوْنَ | *Yusqawna* | they are given to drink |
| مِن رَّحِيق | *min raḥīqin* | from pure wine |
| مَّخْتُومٍ | *makhtūm(in)* | sealed |
| ٢٦-خِتَـٰمُهُۥ مِسْكٌ | *Khitāmu-hū misk(un)* | the seals of it (will be) of musk |
| وَفِى ذَٰلِكَ | *wa-fī dhālika* | and for this |
| فَلْيَتَنَافَس | *fa-l-yatanāfasi* | let those strive, let those aspire |
| ٱلْمُتَنَـٰفِسُونَ | *'al-mutanāfisūn(a)* | who have aspirations |
| ٢٧-وَمِزَاجُهُۥ | *wa-mizāju-hū* | and its mixture (is) |
| مِن تَسْنِيمٍ | *min Tasnīm(in)* | of heavenly fountain, opulence |
| ٢٨-عَيْنًا يَشْرَبُ | *'ainan yashrabu* | A spring ( from the waters) whereof drink |
| بِهَا ٱلْمُقَرَّبُونَ | *bi-ha-(a)l-muqarrabūn(a)* | with it those nearest to Allah |
| ٢٩- إِنَّ ٱلَّذِينَ | *'Inna (a)lladhīna* | Indeed! those |
| أَجْرَمُواْ كَانُواْ | *'ajramū kānū* | guilty were |
| مِنَ ٱلَّذِينَ | *mina (a)lladhīna* | at those |
| ءَامَنُواْ | *'āmanū* | who believed |
| يَضْحَكُونَ | *yadḥakūn(a)* | used to laugh, laughed |
| ٣٠-وَإِذَا مَرُّواْ | *wa-'idha marrū* | And when passed |
| بِهِمْ | *bi-him* | by them |
| يَتَغَامَزُونَ | *yataghāmazūn(a)* | used to wink, winked |
| ٣١-وَإِذَا ٱنقَلَبُوٓاْ | *Wa-'idha-(i)nqalabū* | And when they returned |
| إِلَىٰٓ أَهْلِهِمُ | *'ilā 'ahli-him(u)* | to their people, family |
| انْقَلَبُواْ | *'inqalabū* | they returned |
| فَكِهِينَ | *fakihīn(a)* | jesting, laughing |

| | | |
|---|---|---|
| ٣٢-وَإِذَا رَأَوْهُمْ | *Wa-'idhā ra'aw-hum* | And when they saw them |
| قَالُوٓاْ إِنَّ | *qālu 'inna* | said indeed |
| هَٰٓؤُلَآءِ لَضَآلُّونَ | *hā'ulā'i la-ḍāllūn(a)* | these people (are) have gone astray |
| ٣٣-وَمَآ أُرْسِلُواْ | *Wa-mā 'ursilū* | And they were not sent |
| عَلَيْهِمْ حَٰفِظِينَ | *'alai-him ḥāfiẓīn(a)* | on them as keepers |
| ٣٤-فَٱلْيَومَ | *Fa-l-yawma* | But on this Day |
| ٱلَّذِينَ ءَامَنُواْ | *'alladhīna 'āmanū* | Those who believe |
| مِنَ ٱلْكُفَّارِ | *mina-(a)l-kuffāri* | at the non-believers |
| يَضْحَكُونَ | *yaḍḥakūn(a)* | laugh at |
| ٣٥-عَلَى ٱلأَرَآئِكِ | *'ala 'al-'arā'iki* | On high couches |
| يَنْظُرُونَ | *yanẓurūn(a)* | looking, gazing |
| ٣٦- هَلْ ثُوِّبَ | *Hal thuwwiba* | Are they not paid for |
| اَلْكُفَّارُ | *'al-kuffāru* | the *kuffār*, the non-believers |
| مَا كَانُوا يَفْعَلُونَ | *mā kānū yaf'alūn(a)* | for what they did ? |

*Lesson 16*

سُورَةُ الانفِطَار

آياتها ١٩ — ترتيبها ٨٢

# *AL-'INFIṬĀR, 82:1-19*

## THE CLEAVING ASUNDER / THE CLEAVING

**Revealed in Makkah**

---

<u>**INTRODUCTION**</u>:

This is one of the early Makkan *Suwar* related in the subject matter with *Sūrah Al-'In<u>sh</u>iqāq* 84 and *Sūrah At-Takwīr* 81. It deals with the situation of the Day of Judgment and advises us to prepare ourselves for that Day before it is too late.

| <u>**TRANSLITERATION**</u>: | <u>**ARABIC TEXT**</u>: |
|---|---|
| *Bismillāhi-(a)r-Raḥmāni-(a)r-Raḥīm(i)* | بِسْمِ اللهِ الرَّحْمٰنِ الرَّحِيْمِ |
| 1. *'I<u>dh</u>a-(a)s-samā'u-(a)n-faṭarat* | -إِذَا السَّمَآءُ انْفَطَرَتْ ۝ |
| 2. *Wa 'i<u>dh</u>a-(a)l-kawākibu-(a)n-ta<u>th</u>arat* | -وَإِذَا الْكَوَاكِبُ انْتَثَرَتْ ۝ |
| 3. *Wa 'i<u>dh</u>a-(a)l-biḥāru fujjirat* | -وَإِذَا الْبِحَارُ فُجِّرَتْ ۝ |
| 4. *Wa 'i<u>dh</u>a-(a)l-qubūru bu'<u>th</u>irat* | -وَإِذَا الْقُبُوْرُ بُعْثِرَتْ ۝ |
| 5. *'Alimat nafsun mā qaddamat wa 'a<u>khkh</u>arat* | -عَلِمَتْ نَفْسٌ مَّا قَدَّمَتْ وَأَخَّرَتْ ۝ |
| 6. *Yā 'ayyuha-(a)l-'insānu mā <u>gh</u>arra-ka bi-Rabbi-ka-(a)l-Karīm(i)* | -يٰٓأَيُّهَا الْإِنْسَانُ مَا غَرَّكَ بِرَبِّكَ الْكَرِيْمِ ۝ |
| 7. *'Alla<u>dh</u>ī <u>kh</u>alaqa-ka fa-sawwā-ka fa-'adala-k(a)* | -الَّذِيْ خَلَقَكَ فَسَوّٰىكَ فَعَدَلَكَ ۝ |
| 8. *Fī 'ayyi ṣūratin mā-<u>sh</u>ā'a rakkaba-k(a)* | -فِيْٓ أَيِّ صُوْرَةٍ مَّا شَآءَ رَكَّبَكَ ۝ |
| 9. *Kallā bal tuka<u>dhdh</u>ibūna bi-(a)d-dīn(i)* | -كَلَّا بَلْ تُكَذِّبُوْنَ بِالدِّيْنِ ۝ |
| 10. *Wa 'inna 'alai-kum la-ḥāfiẓīn(a)* | -وَإِنَّ عَلَيْكُمْ لَحٰفِظِيْنَ ۝ |
| 11. *Kirāman Kātibīn(a)* | -كِرَامًا كَاتِبِيْنَ ۝ |

| | |
|---|---|
| 12. *Ya'lamūna mā taf'alūn(a)* | يَعْلَمُونَ مَا تَفْعَلُونَ ۝ |
| 13. *'Inna-(a)l-'abrāra la-fī na'īm(in)* | إِنَّ الْأَبْرَارَ لَفِي نَعِيمٍ ۝ |
| 14. *Wa 'inna-(a)l- fujjāra la-fī jaḥīm(in)* | وَإِنَّ الْفُجَّارَ لَفِي جَحِيمٍ ۝ |
| 15. *Yaṣlawna-hā yawma-(a)d-dīn(i)* | يَصْلَوْنَهَا يَوْمَ الدِّينِ ۝ |
| 16. *Wa mā hum 'an-hā bighā'ibīn(a)* | وَمَا هُمْ عَنْهَا بِغَائِبِينَ ۝ |
| 17. *Wa mā 'adrā-ka mā yawmu-(a)d-dīn(i)* | وَمَا أَدْرَاكَ مَا يَوْمُ الدِّينِ ۝ |
| 18. *Thumma mā 'adrā-ka mā yawmu-(a)d-dīn(i)* | ثُمَّ مَا أَدْرَاكَ مَا يَوْمُ الدِّينِ ۝ |
| 19. *Yawma lā tamliku nafsun li-nafsin* | يَوْمَ لَا تَمْلِكُ نَفْسٌ لِنَفْسٍ |
| *shai'a wa-(a)l-'amru yawma'idhin li-(A)llāh(i)* | شَيْئًا وَالْأَمْرُ يَوْمَئِذٍ لِلَّهِ ۝ |

**TRANSLATIONS:**

In the name of Allāh, Most Gracious,
Most Merciful.

1. When the Sky is cleft asunder;
2. When the stars are scattered;
3. When the Oceans are suffered to burst forth;
4. And when the Graves
   are turned upside down;
5. (Then) shall each soul know what it
   has sent forward and (what it has) kept back.
6. O man! what has seduced you
   from your Lord Most Beneficent?
7. Him Who created you. Fashioned you in
   due proportion, and gave you a just bias;
8. In whatever Form He wills,
   does He put you together.
9. No! But you do reject Right and judgment;

In the name of Allāh, the Beneficent,
the Merciful.

1. When the heaven is cleft asunder,
2. When the planets are dispersed,
3. When the seas are poured forth,
4. And the sepulchers
   are overturned,
5. A soul will know what it
   has sent before (it) and what left behind.
6. O man! what has made you careless
   concerning your Lord, the Bountiful,
7. Who created you, then fashioned,
   then proportioned you?
8. Into whatsoever form He wills,
   He castes you.
9. Nay, but they deny the Judgment:

10. But truly over you
(are appointed angels) to protect you,
11. Kind and Honorable,
writing down (your deeds)
12. They know (and understand) all that you do.
13. As for Righteous, they
will be in Bliss.
14. And the Wicked
they will be in the Fire,
15. Which they will enter on the
Day of Judgment,
16. And they will not be able
to keep away from it.
17. And what will explain to you
what the Day of Judgment is?
18. Again , what will explain to you
what the Day of Judgment is?
19. (It will be) the Day when no soul shall have
power ( to do) anything for another; For the
command, that Day will be (wholly)
with Allāh.

10. Lo! there are above you
guardians,
11. Generous and
recording,
12. Who know (all) that you do.
13. Lo! the righteous verily
will be in delight.
14. And lo! the wicked
verily will be in hell;
15. They will burn therein on the
Day of Judgment,
16. And will not be
absent hence.
17. Ah, what will convey to you
what the Day of Judgment is!
18. Again, what will convey to you
what the Day of Judgment is!
19. A day on which no soul has
power at all for any (other) soul. The
(absolute) command on that Day
is Allāh's.

---

**EXPLANATION:**

82:1-4. The first four *'Āyāt* describe the coming of the Day of Judgment, when the old world order will collapse, giving way to the new. The Heaven will split asunder and the entire cosmology will change and hidden secrets of the Heavens will become known (v. 1). The stars and oceans and other natural phenomena will abandon their natural courses (v. 2-3). The graves will be upturned and the dead will come out alive (v. 4).

82.5. Then, will the Day of Judgment be established, and each soul will come to know all its deeds, good or bad. During this life, whatever actions human beings perform are recorded and sent forth. However, there are some actions which continue until the Day of Judgment, such as any *Ṣadaqah Jāriyah* or evil action, whose effects continue even after the individual's death.

82:6-12. Man is a very tiny portion of Allāh's Creation, yet he is excessively proud of himself. In his pride, he denies the truth of Revelation and the Day of Judgment. Allāh سبحانه وتعالى has created man and fashioned him in the womb of his mother. He has given everyone a form of His choice, and no one has any control over it (v. 7-9).

82:10-12. Human beings, in their pride, may deny the Day of Judgment, but Allāh سبحانه وتعالى has appointed *Kirāman Kātibīn,* the two Angels, who record every thing, good or bad word or action for each individual. The Angel on the right notes the good actions while the Angel on the left notes the bad actions. On the Day of Judgment, these records will be presented to each individual so that he may see for himself all that he did.

82:13-16. There will be a clear division between the wicked and the righteous on the Day of Judgment. The righteous will be happy as they enter the bliss of *Jannah,* while the wicked will be unhappy as they enter the Fire.

82:17-19. These *'Āyāt* emphasize the importance of the Day of Judgment, by twice asking the question, "*What will explain to you what the Day of Judgment is*? (v. 17-18)." Then the Qur'ān answers the question emphatically: that will be the Day of absolute Sovereignty of Allāh سبحانه وتعالى . All our power, resources and connections will be of no avail. It will be the Power and Mercy of Allāh سبحانه وتعالى that will decide the fate of the people.

**<u>WE HAVE LEARNED</u>:**

* Human beings are one of the creations of Allāh سبحانه وتعالى, yet many of them deny Him.
* The two angels *Kirāman Kātibīn,* are writing whatever we do in this life.
* In the *'Ākhirah* all power will belong to Allāh سبحانه وتعالى.

## VOCABULARY

### ٨٢-سُورَةُ ٱلْأَنْفِطَارِ

| | | |
|---|---|---|
| ١-إِذَا ٱلسَّمَاءُ | *'Idhā (a)s-samā'u* | When the Heaven, Sky |
| ٱنفَطَرَتْ | *'infaṭarat* | is cleft asunder, is broken up |
| ٢-وَإِذَا ٱلْكَوَاكِبُ | *Wa-'idha-(a)l-kawākib(u)* | And when the stars, planets |
| ٱنتَثَرَتْ | *'intatharat* | dispersed, scattered |
| ٣-وَإِذَا ٱلْبِحَارُ | *Wa-'idha-(a)l-biḥāru* | And when the seas |
| فُجِّرَتْ | *fujjirat* | burst forth, poured forth |
| ٤-وَإِذَا ٱلْقُبُورُ | *Wa-'idha-(a)l-qubūru* | And when the graves |
| بُعْثِرَتْ | *bu'thirat* | overturned, turned upside down |
| ٥-عَلِمَتْ نَفْسٌ | *'Alimat nafsun* | (then) shall each soul know |
| مَّا قَدَّمَتْ | *mā qaddamat* | what it sent forward |
| وَأَخَّرَتْ | *wa-'akhkharat* | and kept behind |
| ٦-يَـٰٓأَيُّهَا ٱلْإِنسَـٰنُ | *Ya 'ayyuha-(a)l-'Insānu* | O Man, O Humankind |
| مَا غَرَّكَ | *ma gharra-ka* | what seduced you, made you careless |
| بِرَبِّكَ ٱلْكَرِيمِ | *bi-Rabbi-ka-(a)l-Karīm(i)* | from your Lord, the Most Beneficent, the Bountiful |
| ٧-ٱلَّذِى خَلَقَكَ | *'alladhī khalaqa-ka* | He Who created you |
| فَسَوَّىٰكَ | *fa-sawwā-ka* | then fashioned you |
| فَعَدَلَكَ | *fa-'adala-ka* | then proportioned you |
| ٨-فِىٓ أَىِّ صُورَةٍ | *Fi 'ayyi ṣūratin* | In whatever form |
| مَّا شَآءَ رَكَّبَكَ | *mā shā'a rakkaba-k(a)* | He wills, He casts you, He puts you together |
| ٩-كَلَّا بَلْ تُكَذِّبُونَ | *Kalla bal tukadhdhibūna* | Nay but you reject, deny |
| بِٱلدِّينِ | *bi-(a)d-Dīn(i)* | the Judgment |

| | | |
|---|---|---|
| ١٠-وَإِنَّ عَلَيْكُمْ | *Wa-'inna 'alai-kum* | And indeed! over you |
| لَحَـٰفِظِينَ | *la-ḥafiẓīn(a)* | (are angels) to protect you |
| ١١-كِرَامًا كَـٰتِبِينَ | *Kirāman Kātibīn(a)* | The Honorable Recorders ( of your deeds ) |
| ١٢-يَعْلَمُونَ | *ya'lamūna* | They know |
| مَا تَفْعَلُونَ | *ma taf'alūn(a)* | what you do |
| ١٣-إِنَّ ٱلْأَبْرَارَ | *'Inna-(a)-l-'abrāra* | Indeed, the righteous |
| لَفِى نَعِيمٍ | *la-fī na'īm(in)* | will be in bliss, |
| ١٤-وَإِنَّ ٱلْفُجَّارَ | *Wa-'inna-(a)-l-fujjāra* | And indeed the wicked |
| لَفِى جَحِيمٍ | *la-fī jaḥīm(in)* | will be in the fire |
| ١٥-يَصْلَوْنَهَا | *Yaṣlawna-hā* | They will, burn therein |
| يَوْمَ ٱلدِّينِ | *Yawma-(a)d-Dīn(i)* | on the Day of Judgment |
| ١٦-وَمَا هُمْ | *Wa-mā hum* | And they will not be |
| عَنْهَا بِغَائِبِينَ | *'an-ha bi-ghā'ibīn(a)* | absent from it, to keep away therefrom |
| ١٧-وَمَآ أَدْرَىٰكَ | *Wa-mā 'adrā-ka* | And what will explain to you |
| مَا يَوْمُ ٱلدِّينِ | *mā Yawmu-(a)d-Dīn(i)* | What the Day of Judgment is |
| ١٨-ثُمَّ مَآ أَدْرَىٰكَ | *Thuma mā 'adrā-ka* | And what will explain to you |
| مَا يَوْمُ ٱلدِّينِ | *mā Yawmu-(a)d-Dīni* | What the Day of Judgment is |
| ١٩-يَوْمَ لَا تَمْلِكُ | *Yawma lā tamliku* | The Day when not have power |
| نَفْسٌ لِّنَفْسٍ | *nafsun li-nafsin* | a soul for another soul |
| شَيْـًٔا | *shai'an* | anything |
| وَٱلْأَمْرُ | *wa-(a)l-'Amru* | And the Command |
| يَوْمَئِذٍ لِّلَّهِ | *yawma'idhin li-(A)llāh(i)* | That Day belongs to Allah |

**Lesson 17**

سُورَةُ التَّكْوِيرِ — آياتها ٢٩ — ترتيبها ٨١

# *AT-TAKWĪR, 81:1-14*

## THE FOLDING UP / THE OVERTHROWING

**Revealed in Makkah**

---

**INTRODUCTION:**

This is one of the earliest Makkan *Suwar*, and is either sixth or seventh in the chronological order of Revelation.

The *Sūrah* starts with a graphic description of the dissolution of the world before the Day of Judgment, and then speaks about the Day of Judgment itself; at which time, every soul will know what it did in this world. It reaffirms in clear terms that the message of the Qur'ān is from Allāh ﷻ and that Rasūlullāh's ﷺ experience of seeing Angel Jibrīl ﷺ was indeed a true one.

| **TRANSLITERATION:** | **ARABIC TEXT:** |
|---|---|
| *Bismillāhi-(a)r-Raḥmāni-(a)r-Raḥīm(i)* | بِسْمِ اللَّهِ الرَّحْمَٰنِ الرَّحِيمِ |
| 1. *'Idha-(a)sh-shamsu kuwwirat* | -إِذَا الشَّمْسُ كُوِّرَتْ ۝ |
| 2. *Wa 'idha-(a)n-nujūmu-(a)n-kadarat* | -وَإِذَا النُّجُومُ انْكَدَرَتْ ۝ |
| 3. *Wa 'idha-(a)l-jibālu suyyirat* | -وَإِذَا الْجِبَالُ سُيِّرَتْ ۝ |
| 4. *Wa 'idha-(a)l-'ishāru 'uṭṭilat* | -وَإِذَا الْعِشَارُ عُطِّلَتْ ۝ |
| 5. *Wa 'idha-(a)l-wuḥūshu ḥushirat* | -وَإِذَا الْوُحُوشُ حُشِرَتْ ۝ |
| 6. *Wa 'idha-(a)l-biḥāru sujjirat* | -وَإِذَا الْبِحَارُ سُجِّرَتْ ۝ |
| 7. *Wa 'idha-(a)n-nufūsu zuwwijat* | -وَإِذَا النُّفُوسُ زُوِّجَتْ ۝ |
| 8. *Wa 'idha-(a)l-maw'ūdatu su'ilat* | -وَإِذَا الْمَوْءُودَةُ سُئِلَتْ ۝ |
| 9. *Bi-'ayyi dhambin qutilat* | -بِأَيِّ ذَنْبٍ قُتِلَتْ ۝ |

10. *Wa 'idha-(a)ṣ-ṣuḥufu nushirat* — -وَإِذَا الصُّحُفُ نُشِرَتْ ۝

11. *Wa 'idha-(a)s-samā'u kushitat* — -وَإِذَا السَّمَآءُ كُشِطَتْ ۝

12. *Wa 'idha-(a)l-jaḥīmu su''irat* — -وَإِذَا الْجَحِيمُ سُعِّرَتْ ۝

13. *Wa 'idha-(a)l-jannatu 'uzlifat* — -وَإِذَا الْجَنَّةُ أُزْلِفَتْ ۝

14. *'Alimat nafsun mā 'aḥḍarat* — -عَلِمَتْ نَفْسٌ مَّآ أَحْضَرَتْ ۝

**TRANSLATIONS:**

In the name of Allāh, Most Gracious,
Most Merciful.

1. When the Sun (with its spacious light) is folded up;
2. When the stars fall, losing their lustre;
3. When the mountains vanish (like a mirage);
4. When the she-camel, ten months with young, are left untended;
5. When the wild beasts are herded together (in human habitations):
6. When the oceans boil over with a swell;
7. When the souls are sorted out, (being joined, like with like);
8. When the female (infant), buried alive, is questioned-
9. For what crime she was killed;
10. When the Scrolls are laid open;
11. When the World on High is unveiled;
12. When the Blazing Fire is kindled to fierce heat;
13. And when the Garden is brought near;
14. Then shall each soul know what it has put forward.

In the name of Allāh, the Beneficent,
the Merciful.

1. When the sun is overthrown,
2. And when the stars fall,
3. And when the hills are moved,
4. And when the camels big with young are abandoned,
5. And when the wild beasts are herded together,
6. And when the seas rise,
7. And when the souls are reunited,
8. And when the girl-child that was buried alive is asked
9. For what sin she was slain.
10. And when the pages are laid open,
11. And when the sky is torn away,
12. And when hell is lighted,
13. And when the garden is brought nigh,
14. (Then) every soul will know what it has made ready.

**EXPLANATION**:

81:1-6. These verses describe the breakup of the world, in which the natural order of the cosmos will fall apart. The sun, the stars and the mountains will collapse; the oceans will overflow, putting the world into complete disorder (v. 1-3, 6).

On that day, a ten-month old, pregnant she-camel will be left unattended by its owners. In Arabia, a pregnant she-camel about to deliver was considered a most prized possession. Abandoning such a precious possession on that Day underlines the great catastrophic impact of this experience. On that Day, a man will not care for his wealth, possessions or dear ones (v. 4).

During a calamity, animals herd together, forgetting their inbred hostility towards one another. On that Day, animals and humans will all come together, not hurting one another, each individual being worried about himself (v. 5).

81:7. On the Day of Judgment, bodies will be united with souls. Human beings will be resurrected once again (v. 7).

81:8-9. The Arabs were deeply ashamed of fathering a girl, and it was common practice to bury newborn females alive. Islam not only banned this inhuman custom, it raised the status of women to a very high level. An infant child on that Day will be asked why she was killed. Her killers will be brought to justice on that Day. Thus, the Arabs were not only admonished for the evil and barbaric custom they advocated, they were warned of its consequences on the Day of Judgment.

81:10-14. It will be the dawn of a new day. The Books of Actions will be opened. The Heavens will reveal its secrets, the Fire of Hell will blaze, ready to receive the evil-doers and the *Jannah* will be made ready and visible to the righteous (v. 10-13). Every soul on that Day will know whatever good or bad it did during its life in this world (v. 14).

**WE HAVE LEARNED**:
* On the Day of Judgment the entire cosmic order would change and a new order will take shape.
* The parents who killed or abused their children will be held accountable for their actions.
* Every soul will come to know what actions it did in this world.

**VOCABULARY**

٨١-سُورَةُ ٱلتَّكْوِير

| | | |
|---|---|---|
| ١-إِذَا ٱلشَّمْسُ كُوِّرَتْ | *'Idha-(a)sh-shamsu kuwwirat* | When the sun (is) folded up, overthrown |
| ٢-وَإِذَا ٱلنُّجُومُ | *Wa-'idha-(a)n-nujūmu* | And when the stars |
| ٱنكَدَرَتْ | *'inkadarat* | fall (losing their luster) |
| ٣-وَإِذَا ٱلْجِبَالُ | *Wa-'idha-(a)l-jibālu* | And when the mountains |

| | | |
|---|---|---|
| سُيِّرَتْ | *suyyirat* | are blown up, vanish |
| ٤-وَإِذَا ٱلْعِشَارُ | *Wa-'idha-(a)l-'ishāru* | And when the she-camels |
| عُطِّلَتْ | *'uṭṭilat* | are abandoned, left unattended |
| ٥- وَإِذَا ٱلْوُحُوشُ | *Wa-'idha-(a)l-wuḥūshu* | And when the wild beasts |
| حُشِرَتْ | *ḥushirat* | are herded together |
| ٦-وَإِذَا ٱلْبِحَارُ | *Wa-'idha-(a)l-biḥāru* | And when the oceans, the seas |
| سُجِّرَتْ | *sujjirat* | boil over with a swell, rise |
| ٧-وَإِذَا ٱلنُّفُوسُ | *Wa-'idha-(a)n-nūfusu* | And when the souls |
| زُوِّجَتْ | *zuwwijat* | (are) reunited |
| ٨-وَإِذَا ٱلْمَوْءُودَةُ | *Wa-'idha-(a)l-maw'ūdatu* | And when the buried alive female infant |
| سُئِلَتْ | *su'ilat* | is asked |
| ٩-بِأَيِّ ذَنبٍ | *Bi-'ayyi dhanbin* | For what sin |
| قُتِلَتْ | *qutilat* | was she slain |
| ١٠-وَإِذَا ٱلصُّحُفُ | *Wa-'idha-(a)ṣ-ṣuḥufu* | And when the records, the pages |
| نُشِرَتْ | *nushirat* | are laid open |
| ١١-وَإِذَا ٱلسَّمَآءُ | *Wa-'idha-(a)s-samā'u* | And when the sky |
| كُشِطَتْ | *kushiṭat* | is unveiled, is torn away |
| ١٢-وَإِذَا ٱلْجَحِيمُ | *Wa-'idha-(a)l-Jaḥīmu* | And when the Hell,the blazing fire |
| سُعِّرَتْ | *su''irat* | is kindled |
| ١٣-وَإِذَا ٱلْجَنَّةُ | *Wa-'idha-(a)l-Jannatu* | And when the *Jannah*, the Garden |
| أُزْلِفَتْ | *'uzlifat* | is brought near |
| ١٤-عَلِمَتْ نَفْسٌ | *'alimat nafsun* | will know a soul |
| مَّآ أَحْضَرَتْ | *mā 'aḥḍarat* | what it put forth |

*Lesson 18*

# *AT-TAKWĪR, 81:15-29*

## THE FOLDING UP / THE OVERTHROWING

**Revealed in Makkah**

---

| **TRANSLITERATION:** | **ARABIC TEXT:** |
|---|---|
| 15. *Fa-lā 'uqsimu bi-(a)l-khunnas(i)* | -فَلَآ أُقْسِمُ بِالْخُنَّسِ ۝ |
| 16. *'Al-jawāri-(a)l-kunnas(i)* | -الْجَوَارِ الْكُنَّسِ ۝ |
| 17. *Wa-(a)l-laili 'idhā 'as'as(a)* | -وَالَّيْلِ إِذَا عَسْعَسَ ۝ |
| 18. *Wa-(a)s-subhi 'idhā tanaffas(a)* | -وَالصُّبْحِ إِذَا تَنَفَّسَ ۝ |
| 19. *'Inna-hū la-qawlu Rasūlin Karīm(in)* | -إِنَّهُ لَقَوْلُ رَسُولٍ كَرِيمٍ ۝ |
| 20. *Dhī quwwatin 'inda Dhi-(a)l-'Arshi makīn(in)* | -ذِي قُوَّةٍ عِندَ ذِي الْعَرْشِ مَكِينٍ ۝ |
| 21. *Muṭā'in thamma 'amīn(in)* | -مُّطَاعٍ ثَمَّ أَمِينٍ ۝ |
| 22. *Wa mā ṣāḥibu-kum bi-majnūn(in)* | -وَمَا صَاحِبُكُم بِمَجْنُونٍ ۝ |
| 23. *Wa laqad ra'āhu bi-(a)l-'ufuqi-(a)l-mubīn(i)* | -وَلَقَدْ رَآهُ بِالْأُفُقِ الْمُبِينِ ۝ |
| 24. *Wa mā huwa 'ala-(a)l-ghaibi bi-ḍanīn(in)* | -وَمَا هُوَ عَلَى الْغَيْبِ بِضَنِينٍ ۝ |
| 25. *Wa mā huwa bi-qawli Shaiṭāni(n)-r-Rajīm(in)* | -وَمَا هُوَ بِقَوْلِ شَيْطَٰنٍ رَّجِيمٍ ۝ |
| 26. *Fa-'aina tadhhabūn(a)* | -فَأَيْنَ تَذْهَبُونَ ۝ |
| 27. *'In huwa 'illā dhikrun li-(a)l-'ālamīn(a)* | -إِنْ هُوَ إِلَّا ذِكْرٌ لِّلْعَٰلَمِينَ ۝ |
| 28. *Li-man shā'a min-kum an-yastaqīm(a)* | -لِمَن شَآءَ مِنكُمْ أَن يَسْتَقِيمَ ۝ |
| 29. *Wa mā tashā'ūna 'illā 'an-yashā'* | -وَمَا تَشَآءُونَ إِلَّآ أَن يَشَآءَ |
| *'Allāhu Rabbu-(a)l-'Ālamīn(a)* | اللَّهُ رَبُّ الْعَٰلَمِينَ ۝ |

**TRANSLATIONS**:

15. So truly I call to witness
the planets that recede,
16. Go straight, or hide;
17. And the night as it dissipates;
18. And the Dawn as it breathes
away the darkness;
19. Truly this is the word of a most
honorable Messenger,
20. Endued with Power,
with rank before the Lord of the Throne,
21. With authority there,
(And) faithful to his trust
22. And (O People) your companion
is not one possessed;
23. And without doubt he saw him
in the clear horizon.
24. Neither does he withhold grudgingly
a knowledge of the unseen.
25. Nor is it the word of an
evil spirit accursed.
26. Then where are you going?
27. Truly this is no less than a Message
to (all) the Worlds:
28. (With profit) to whoever among you wills
to go straight
29. But you shall not will
Except as Allāh wills,
The Cherisher of the Worlds.

15. Oh, but I call to
witness the planets
16. The stars which rise and set,
17. And the close of night
18. And the breath of morning;
19. That this is in truth the word of an
honoured messenger,
20. Mighty, established in the presence
of the Lord of the Throne,
21. (One) to be obeyed,
and trustworthy
22. And your comrade
is not mad.
23. Surely he beheld him
on the clear horizon.
24. And he is not avid
of the Unseen.
25. Nor is this utterance of a
devil worthy to be stoned:
26. Whither then go you?
27. This is naught else than a reminder
to creation,
28. To whomsoever of you will
to walk straight.
29. And you will not,
unless (it be) that Allāh,
the Lord of Creation, wills.

**EXPLANATION**:

81:15-20. Allāh سبحانه وتعالى swears by the Planets, the Night and the Dawn, to emphasize that the Qur'ān is the Authoritative Word of Allāh سبحانه وتعالى, brought to Rasūlullāh ﷺ by the generous Messenger, Angel Jibrīl عليه السلام. Angel Jibrīl عليه السلام has been given great power and authority by Allāh سبحانه وتعالى, the Lord and Owner of all Power and Glory. His authority is well respected and He is a trustworthy Messenger. Thus Angel Jibrīl عليه السلام delivers the message exactly as it is entrusted to him by Allāh سبحانه وتعالى.

81:21-25. Many *Kuffār* denied the authenticity of the Qur'ān, and claimed that Rasūlullāh ﷺ was possessed by the *Jinns*. Allāh سبحانه وتعالى affirms that the Qur'ān is indeed authentic; that the messenger Jibrīl عليه السلام is reliable and that Rasūlullāh ﷺ was well known to the people as being *Al-'Amīn* (Trustworthy) and *As-Sādiq* (the Truthful).

These visitations by Angel Jibrīl عليه السلام to Rasūlullāh ﷺ were not visions or imaginary happenings. Rasūlullāh ﷺ saw the Angel عليه السلام with his own eyes and in full possession of all his senses. According to tradition and the Qur'ānic verification, Rasūlullāh ﷺ saw Angel Jibrīl عليه السلام in his own form twice: once on the horizon, the night of first Revelation in the cave of *Ḥirā*, and another time on the Night of *Mi'rāj*, the Ascension (see *Sūrah Al-Isrā'* 17:1).

Rasūlullāh ﷺ received the Message and delivered it to the people exactly as he received it. Neither did he withhold any information nor did he add anything to it (v. 24). Such an Authentic Message cannot come from the *Shaiṭān*, cursed and condemned by Allāh سبحانه وتعالى. In addition, the noble Message of the Qur'ān and the pure life of Rasūlullāh ﷺ testified to the Truth of the Message.

81:26-29. Thus, the Authentic Message, brought by a reliable messenger, is here for us. Where do we now turn away and go? The Message which Allāh سبحانه وتعالى in His infinite wisdom, sent to the Makkans originally, is meant for the entire universe to follow. It is the Word of the Creator of the Universe, and is designed to benefit all human beings. However, it is the choice of humans to accept it or to reject it. If the human heart is responsive to the Divine Command, Allāh سبحانه وتعالى shows them the Truth and guides them to the Straight Path. If, on the other hand, one's heart is crooked and not amenable to the Divine Message, Allāh سبحانه وتعالى strengthens the obstinacy of that person.

Ultimately, it is the Will of Allāh سبحانه وتعالى that we must conform to and obey. If we do not care to do so, Allāh سبحانه وتعالى does not need us, and He lets us go astray till the Day of Judgment, when He will raise us and judge us on what we did.

The *Kirāman Kātibīn,* Kind and Honorable Angels, are the two Angels who write down all that we do. Scrolls of their writings will be presented to us on the Day of Judgment.

**WE HAVE LEARNED:**

* The Qur'ān is the authentic Message of Allāh سُبْحَانَهُ وَتَعَالَى.
* It was revealed to Rasūlullāh ﷺ through Angel Jibrīl عَلَيْهِ السَّلَام.
* The message of the Qur'ān and the life of Rasūlullāh ﷺ provide us with guidance to lead a meaningful life.

### VOCABULARY II

### ٨١-سُورَةُ ٱلتَّكْوِير

| | | |
|---|---|---|
| ١٥-فَلَآ أُقْسِمُ | *Fa-lā 'uqsimu* | So,verily I call to witness |
| بِٱلْخُنَّسِ | *bi-(a)l-khunnas(i)* | the planets |
| ١٦-ٱلْجَوَارِ ٱلْكُنَّسِ | *'al-jawāri-(a)l-kunnas(i)* | that move, straight or hide |
| ١٧-وَٱلَّيْلِ | *Wa-(a)l-laili* | And the night |
| إِذَا عَسْعَسَ | *'Idhā 'as'asa* | as it dissipates |
| ١٨-وَٱلصُّبْحِ | *Wa-(a)ṣ-ṣubḥi* | And the morning |
| إِذَا تَنَفَّسَ | *'Idhā tanaffasa* | when it breathes away (the darkness) |
| ١٩-إِنَّهُ | *'Inna-hū* | Indeed, it is |
| لَقَوْلُ | *la-qawlu* | this is a word, a speech |
| رَسُولٍ كَرِيمٍ | *Rasūlin Karīm(in)* | (of) an Honored Messenger |
| ٢٠-ذِى قُوَّةٍ | *Dhi quwwatin* | Possessing power |
| عِنْدَ | *'inda* | in the ( presence) |
| ذِى ٱلْعَرْشِ | *Dhī-(a)l-'Arshi* | the Lord of the Throne |
| مَكِينٍ | *makīn(in)* | established |
| ٢١-مُّطَاعٍ | *Muṭā'in* | One who is obeyed, has authority |
| ثَمَّ أَمِينٍ | *thamma 'amīn(in)* | then is trustworthy, there he is faithful to his trust |
| ٢٢-وَمَا صَاحِبُكُم | *wa-mā ṣāḥibu-kum* | And your friend is not |

| | | |
|---|---|---|
| بِمَجْنُونٍ | *bi-majnūn(in)* | possessed, mad |
| ٢٣-وَلَقَدْ رَءَاهُ | *Wa-laqad ra'ā-hu* | surely, he saw him |
| بِٱلْأُفُقِ ٱلْمُبِينِ | *bi-(a)l-'ufuqi-(a)l-mubīn(i)* | on the clear horizon |
| ٢٤-وَمَا هُوَ | *Wa-mā huwa* | And he is not |
| عَلَى ٱلْغَيْبِ | *'ala -(a)l-ghaibi* | of the unseen |
| بِضَنِينٍ | *bi-ḍanīn(in)* | avid, stingy |
| ٢٥-وَمَا هُوَ | *Wa-mā huwa* | And nor is it |
| بِقَوْلِ | *bi-qawli* | the saying of, the word of |
| شَيْطَٰنٍ رَّجِيمٍ | *Shaiṭāni-r-Rajīm(in)* | a Satan accursed |
| ٢٦-فَأَيْنَ تَذْهَبُونَ | *Fa-'aina tadhhabūn(a)* | So whither you go |
| ٢٧-إِنْ هُوَ | *'In huwa* | This is verily |
| إِلَّا | *'illā* | nothing except |
| ذِكْرٌ لِّلْعَٰلَمِينَ | *dhikrun li-(a)l-'ālamīn(a)* | a message for the Worlds |
| ٢٨-لِمَن شَآءَ | *Li-man shā'a* | for whoever wills |
| مِنكُمْ | *min-kum* | from among you |
| أَن يَسْتَقِيمَ | *'an yastaqīm(a)* | to walk straight, to go straight |
| ٢٩-وَمَا تَشَآءُونَ | *Wa-mā tasha'ūna* | And you do not will |
| إِلَّآ أَنْ | *'Illā 'an* | except as |
| يَشَآءَ ٱللَّهُ | *yashā' 'Allāhu* | Allah wills |
| رَبُّ ٱلْعَٰلَمِينَ | *Rabbu-(a)l-'Ālamīn(a)* | The Lord of the Worlds |

**Lesson 19**

سُورَةُ عَبَسَ

آياتها ٤٢ — ترتيبها ٨٠

# *'ABASA, 80:1-23*

## HE FROWNED / HE FROWNED

**Revealed in Makkah**

---

**INTRODUCTION:**

This is an early Makkan *Sūrah*. It is related to an incident in the life of Rasūlullāh ﷺ. One day, he was preaching to the chiefs of *Quraish* about the Message of Islam. 'Abdullāh ibn Maktūm, a blind man and a commoner, approached Rasūlullāh ﷺ and asked him to teach Islam. Rasūlullāh ﷺ was unhappy with this interruption. Though kind and generous, Rasūlullāh ﷺ felt that if these Makkan chiefs were able to see the Truth, it would bring a tremendous change to the fortunes of Islam and the Muslim community as a whole. In denying 'Abdullāh a hearing, Rasūlullāh ﷺ was motivated by the noblest of sentiments for the cause of Islam. The blind man, however, was hurt.

This *Sūrah* was revealed in criticism of Rasūlullāh's action, and it taught him an important lesson: that guidance was not in the hands of Rasūlullāh ﷺ, but rather in the Hands of Allāh سبحانه وتعالى . He who was eager to learn the Message had more right to Rasūlullāh's ﷺ attention than the non-believing Makkan chiefs did.

This story demonstrates the integrity of Rasūlullāh ﷺ in conveying Allāh's Message. If there was any part of the Divine Message to be hidden from the people it would be these verses. However, without reservation, Rasūlullāh ﷺ communicated this *Sūrah* to his *Ṣaḥābah*, and till this day, it stands as testimony to the honesty and integrity of Rasūlullāh's ﷺ.

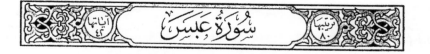

| **TRANSLITERATION:** | **ARABIC TEXT:** |
|---|---|
| *Bismillāhi-(a)r-Raḥmāni-(a)r-Raḥīm(i)* | بِسْمِ اللهِ الرَّحْمٰنِ الرَّحِيْمِ |
| 1. *'Abasa wa-tawallā* | -عَبَسَ وَتَوَلّٰىٓ ۝ |
| 2. *'An jā'ahu-(a)l-'a'mā* | -اَنْ جَآءَهُ الْاَعْمٰى ۝ |
| 3. *Wa mā yudrī-ka la'alla-hū yazzakkā* | -وَمَا يُدْرِيْكَ لَعَلَّهٗ يَزَّكّٰىٓ ۝ |
| 4. *'Aw ya<u>dh</u><u>dh</u>akkaru fa-tanfa'a-hu-(a)<u>dh</u>-<u>dh</u>ikrā* | -اَوْ يَذَّكَّرُ فَتَنْفَعَهُ الذِّكْرٰى ۝ |

| | | |
|---|---|---|
| 5. | *'Ammā mani-('i)staghnā* | -أَمَّا مَنِ اسْتَغْنَىٰ ○ |
| 6. | *Fa-'anta la-hū taṣaddā* | -فَأَنتَ لَهُ تَصَدَّىٰ ○ |
| 7. | *Wa mā 'alai-ka al-lā yazzakkā* | -وَمَا عَلَيْكَ أَلَّا يَزَّكَّىٰ ○ |
| 8. | *Wa 'ammā man jā'aka yas'ā* | -وَأَمَّا مَن جَاءَكَ يَسْعَىٰ ○ |
| 9. | *Wa huwa yakhshā* | -وَهُوَ يَخْشَىٰ ○ |
| 10. | *Fa-'anta 'anhu talahhā* | -فَأَنتَ عَنْهُ تَلَهَّىٰ ○ |
| 11. | *Kallā 'inna-hā tadhkirah(tun)* | -كَلَّا إِنَّهَا تَذْكِرَةٌ ○ |
| 12. | *Fa-man shā'a dhakarah(ū)* | -فَمَن شَاءَ ذَكَرَهُ ○ |
| 13. | *Fī ṣuḥufin mukarramah(tin)* | -فِي صُحُفٍ مُّكَرَّمَةٍ ○ |
| 14. | *Marfū'atin muṭahharah(tin)* | -مَّرْفُوعَةٍ مُّطَهَّرَةٍ ○ |
| 15. | *Bi-'aidī safarah(tin)* | -بِأَيْدِي سَفَرَةٍ ○ |
| 16. | *Kirāmin bararah(tin)* | -كِرَامٍ بَرَرَةٍ ○ |
| 17. | *Qutila-(a)l-'insānu mā 'akfarah(ū)* | -قُتِلَ الْإِنسَانُ مَا أَكْفَرَهُ ○ |
| 18. | *Min 'ayyī shai'in khalaqah(ū)* | -مِنْ أَيِّ شَيْءٍ خَلَقَهُ ○ |
| 19. | *Min nuṭfatin khalaqa-hū fa-qaddara-h(ū)* | -مِن نُّطْفَةٍ خَلَقَهُ فَقَدَّرَهُ ○ |
| 20. | *Thumma-(a)s-sabīla yassarah(ū)* | -ثُمَّ السَّبِيلَ يَسَّرَهُ ○ |
| 21. | *Thumma 'amāta-hū fa-'aqbara-h(ū)* | -ثُمَّ أَمَاتَهُ فَأَقْبَرَهُ ○ |
| 22. | *Thumma 'idhā shā'a 'an-sharah(ū)* | -ثُمَّ إِذَا شَاءَ أَنشَرَهُ ○ |
| 23. | *Kallā lammā yaqḍi mā 'amarah(ū)* | -كَلَّا لَمَّا يَقْضِ مَا أَمَرَهُ ○ |

**TRANSLATIONS:**

In the name of Allāh, Most Gracious,
Most Merciful.

1. (The Prophet) frowned and turned away,
2. Because there came to him the blind man (interrupting).
3. But what could tell you but that perchance he might grow (in spiritual understanding)
4. Or that he might receive admonition, and the teaching might profit him?
5. As to one who regards himself as self-sufficient,
6. To him do you attend;
7. Though it is no blame to you if he grow not (in spiritual understanding).
8. But as to him who came to you striving earnestly,
9. And with fear (in his heart)
10. Of him you were unmindful.
11. By no means (should it be so)! For it is indeed a Message of instruction:
12. Therefore let whoso will, keep it in remembrance.
13. (It is) in books held (greatly) in Honour,
14. Exalted (in dignity), kept pure and holy,
15. (Written) by the hands of scribes
16. Honorable and Pious and just.
17. Woe to man! What has made him reject Allāh?
18. From what stuff has He created him?
19. From a sperm-drop, He has created him, and then molded him in due proportions;
20. Then does He make His path smooth for him;

In the name of Allāh, the Beneficent,
the Merciful.

1. He frowned and turned away
2. Because the blind man came to him.
3. What could inform you but that he might grow (in grace)
4. Or take heed and so the reminder might avail him?
5. As for him who think himself independent,
6. To him you pay regard.
7. Yet it is not your concern if he grow not (in grace).
8. But as for him who come to you with earnest purpose
9. And has fear,
10. From him you are distracted.
11. Nay, but verily it is Admonishment,
12. So let whosoever will pay heed to it,
13. On honoured leaves,
14. Exalted, purified,
15. (Set down) by scribes
16. Noble and righteous.
17. Man is (self-) destroyed: how ungrateful!
18. From what thing does He creates him?
19. From a drop of seed. He create him and proportioned him,
20. Then makes the way easy for him

| | |
|---|---|
| 21. Then He causes him to die, and puts him in his Grave; | 21. Then cause him to die, and bury him; |
| 22. Then, when it is His will, He will raise him up (again) | 22. Then, when He wills, He brings him again to life. |
| 23. By no means has he Fulfilled what Allāh Has commanded him. | 23. Nay, but (man) has not done what He commanded him. |

---

**EXPLANATION:**

80:1-4. 'Abdullāh ibn Maktūm, the blind Makkan commoner, came to Rasūlullāh as he sat with the Makkan chiefs. 'Abdullāh wanted to learn about Islam. He was so eager that he interrupted Rasūlullāh and asked to be taught something from the Message. Rasūlullāh was displeased by this interruption and he turned his attention away from him (v. 1-2).

Rasūlullāh was only a messenger sent by Allāh for the well-being of all humanity. He did not know that the blind man could grow in purity through Islamic faith. The words of Rasūlullāh might have benefitted the blind man more than they could have the Makkan chiefs, since the former was willing to listen. Only Allāh has the Power of guidance and in His Sight, a commoner and a prince are alike; it is their faith that differentiates the two.

80:5-7. Rasūlullāh was busy preaching to the Makkan chiefs, but in their pride, they rejected the Truth of Islam (v. 5-6). It was not in the power of Rasūlullāh or any other human being to purify someone from the impurity of *Kufr*, and to guide him to the pure path of Islam. It is only Allāh who possesses this power.

80:8-10. Compared with the arrogant Makkan chiefs, 'Abdullāh ibn Maktūm came of his own accord, with the fear of Allāh in heart, and eager to learn. Yet Rasūlullāh was not attentive to his call.

80:11-16. The Message of Islam is not for any one special group. It is a Message and Remembrance from Allāh for anyone who wishes to learn and benefit from it (v.11-12). It was written down in several books by pious scribes who were known for the purity of their intentions and for their integrity (v. 13-16). Thus, for the God-fearing, there was every reason to believe in the Message. However, if people did not believe, Rasūlullāh and his followers are not responsible for their disbelief. Allāh guides whomever He wishes to the Truth.

80:17-23. In spite of all the favors of Allāh, man is ungrateful to Him. His actions do not hurt anyone but himself (v. 17). He forgets that it is Allāh who created him from an insignificant drop of seed, proportioned him in his mother's womb, and then brought him to life and eased his way into this world. He will cause him to die, and then bring him back to life (v.18-22).

Human beings have been created with intelligence, and have been given a choice between good and evil. We have been provided with the guidance of *Waḥī*, yet, some do not fulfill the purpose of our creation. Some do not believe and follow the Straight Path (v. 23).

**WE HAVE LEARNED**:

* The guidance is always in the hands of Allāh ﷻ.
* The Qur'ān is a message for everyone whoever wants to pay heed to it.
* Human beings would be held responsible for their actions as they have the freedom to choose the truth or falsehood.

## VOCABULARY

### ٨٠-سُورَةُ عَبَسَ

| | | |
|---|---|---|
| ١-عَبَسَ | *'Abasa* | He frowned |
| وَتَوَلَّىٰ | *wa-tawallā* | and turned away |
| ٢-أَنْ جَآءَهُ | *'An jā'a-hu* | Because came to him |
| اَلأَعْمَىٰ | *'al-'a'mā* | The blind man |
| ٣-وَمَا يُدْرِيْكَ | *Wa-mā yudrī-ka* | And what would tell you |
| لَعَلَّهُ | *la'alla-hū* | But that perchance |
| يَزَّكَّىٰ | *yazzakkā* | he might grow in purity |
| ٤-أَوْ يَذَّكَّرُ | *'Aw yadhdhakkaru* | Or that he might take heed |
| فَتَنْفَعَهُ | *fa-tanfa'a-hu* | so might profit him |
| اَلذِّكْرَىٰ | *'adh-dhikrā* | the Reminder, the teaching |
| ٥-أَمَّا مَنِ | *'Ammā man(i)* | As to the one who |
| اِسْتَغْنَىٰ | *'istaghnā* | who regards himself independent |
| ٦-فَأَنْتَ لَهُ | *Fa-'anta la-hū* | So, you to him |
| تَصَدَّىٰ | *taṣaddā* | pay regard to, attend to |
| ٧-وَمَا عَلَيْكَ | *Wa-mā 'alai-ka* | And it is not your responsibility |
| اَلاَّ يَزَّكَّىٰ | *'alla yazzakkā* | that he does not grow |

| | | |
|---|---|---|
| ٨-وَأَمَّا مَنْ | *Wa-'ammā man* | And as for the one who |
| جَآءَكَ يَسْعَىٰ | *jā'a-ka yas'ā* | came to you striving |
| ٩-وَهُوَ يَخْشَىٰ | *Wa-huwa yakhshā* | And he had fear (in his heart) |
| فَأَنتَ عَنْهُ | *fa-'anta 'an-hu* | you were from him |
| تَلَهَّىٰ | *talahhā* | distracted |
| ١١-كَلاً إِنَّهَا | *Kalla 'inna-hā* | Nay, but indeed it is |
| تَذْكِرَةٌ | *tadhkirah(tun)* | an advice, a message of remembrance |
| ١٢-فَمَنْ شَآءَ | *fa-man shā'a* | So, whosoever will |
| ذَكَرَهُ | *dhakara-h(u)* | pay heed to it |
| ١٣-فِي صُحُفٍ | *Fī ṣuḥufin* | In books |
| مُّكَرَّمَةٍ | *mukarramah(tin)* | held greatly in honor |
| ١٤-مَّرْفُوعَةٍ | *marfū'atin* | Exalted |
| مُّطَهَّرَةٍ | *muṭahhrah(tin)* | purified |
| ١٥-بِأَيْدِي سَفَرَةٍ | *Bi-'aidī safarah(tin)* | (Written) by the hands of scribes |
| ١٦-كِرَامٍ بَرَرَةٍ | *Kirāmin bararah(tin)* | Noble righteous |
| ١٧-قُتِلَ ٱلْإِنسَٰنُ | *qutila-(a)l-'insānu* | self-destroyed is the man, woe to man ! |
| مَآ أَكْفَرَهُ | *mā 'akfara-h(u)* | how ungrateful is he |
| ١٨-مِنْ أَيِّ شَيْءٍ | *Min 'ayyi shai'in* | From what thing |
| خَلَقَهُ | *khalaqa-hu* | He created him |
| ١٩-مِن نُّطْفَةٍ | *Min nuṭfatin* | From a drop of sperm |
| خَلَقَهُ | *khalaqa-hu* | He has created him |
| فَقَدَّرَهُ | *fa-qaddara-hu* | then molded him |

| | | |
|---|---|---|
| ٢٠-ثُمَّ ٱلسَّبِيلَ | *<u>Th</u>umma -(a)s-sabīla* | Then the way |
| يَسَّرَهُ | *yassara-hū* | He makes easy for him |
| ٢١-ثُمَّ أَمَاتَهُ | *<u>Th</u>umma 'amāta-hū* | Then He causes him to die |
| فَأَقْبَرَهُ | *fa-'aqbara-hū* | and puts him in the grave |
| ٢٢-ثُمَّ إِذَا شَآءَ | *<u>Th</u>umma 'i<u>dh</u>ā <u>sh</u>ā'a* | Then when He wills |
| أَنْشَرَهُ | *'an<u>sh</u>ara-h(u)* | raise him up, restore him |
| ٢٣-كَلاَّ لَمَّا يَقْضِ | *kallā lammā yaqḍi* | Nay, but he (man) did not do, did not fulfill |
| مَآ أَمَرَهُ | *mā 'amara-h(u)* | what He commanded him to do |

*Lesson 20*

# *'ABASA, 80:24-42*

## HE FROWNED / HE FROWNED

**Revealed in Makkah**

| **TRANSLITERATION**: | **ARABIC TEXT**: |
|---|---|
| 24. *Fa-(a)l-yanẓur-i-(a)l-'insānu 'ilā ṭa'āmih(ī)* | -فَلْيَنظُرِ الْإِنسَانُ إِلَىٰ طَعَامِهِ |
| 25. *'Annā ṣabab-na-(a)l-mā'a ṣabbā(n)* | -أَنَّا صَبَبْنَا الْمَاءَ صَبًّا |
| 26. *Thumma shaqaq-na-(a)l-'arḍa shaqqā(n)* | -ثُمَّ شَقَقْنَا الْأَرْضَ شَقًّا |
| 27. *Fa-'anbat-nā fī-hā ḥabbā(n)* | -فَأَنبَتْنَا فِيهَا حَبًّا |
| 28. *Wa-'inaban wa-qaḍbā(n)* | -وَعِنَبًا وَقَضْبًا |
| 29. *Wa-zaitūn-an wa-nakhlā(n)* | -وَزَيْتُونًا وَنَخْلًا |
| 30. *Wa-ḥadā'iqa ghulbā(n)* | -وَحَدَائِقَ غُلْبًا |
| 31. *Wa-fākihatan wa-'abbā(n)* | -وَفَاكِهَةً وَأَبًّا |
| 32. *Matā'a-l-la-kum wa-li'an'āmi-kum* | -مَّتَاعًا لَّكُمْ وَلِأَنْعَامِكُمْ |
| 33. *Fa-'idhā jā'ati-(a)ṣ-Ṣākhkhah(tu)* | -فَإِذَا جَاءَتِ الصَّاخَّةُ |
| 34. *Yawma yafirru-(a)l-mar'u min 'akhīh(i)* | -يَوْمَ يَفِرُّ الْمَرْءُ مِنْ أَخِيهِ |
| 35. *Wa-'ummi-hī wa-'abīh(i)* | -وَأُمِّهِ وَأَبِيهِ |
| 36. *Wa-ṣāḥibati-hī wa-banīh(i)* | -وَصَاحِبَتِهِ وَبَنِيهِ |
| 37. *Li-kulli-(a)mri'in min-hum yawma'idhin sha'nu(n)-y-yughnīh(i)* | -لِكُلِّ امْرِئٍ مِّنْهُمْ يَوْمَئِذٍ شَأْنٌ يُغْنِيهِ |
| 38. *Wujūhun yawma'idhin musfirah(tun)* | -وُجُوهٌ يَوْمَئِذٍ مُّسْفِرَةٌ |

39. *Ḍāḥikat-un mustabshirah(tun)* -ضَاحِكَةٌ مُّسْتَبْشِرَةٌ ۝

40. *Wa-wujūhun yawma'idhin 'alai-hā ghabarah(tun)* -وَوُجُوهٌ يَوْمَئِذٍ عَلَيْهَا غَبَرَةٌ ۝

41. *Tarhaqu-hā qatarah(tun)* -تَرْهَقُهَا قَتَرَةٌ ۝

42. *'Ulā'ika humu-(a)l-kafaratu-(a)l-fajarah(tu)* -أُولَٰئِكَ هُمُ الْكَفَرَةُ الْفَجَرَةُ ۝

**TRANSLATIONS:**

| | |
|---|---|
| 24. Then let man look at<br>his Food (And how We provide it): | 24. Let man consider<br>his food: |
| 25. For that We pour forth water in abundance | 25. How We pour water in showers |
| 26. And We split the earth in fragments | 26. Then split the earth in clefts |
| 27. And produce therein Corn, | 27. And cause the grain to grow therein |
| 28. And Grapes and nutritious Plants, | 28. And grapes and green fodder |
| 29. And Olives and Dates, | 29. And olive-trees and palm-trees |
| 30. And enclosed Gardens,<br>Dense with lofty trees | 30. And garden-closes<br>of thick foliage |
| 31. And Fruits and Fodder- | 31. And fruits and grasses: |
| 32. For use and convenience to you<br>and your cattle | 32. Provision for you<br>and your cattle |
| 33. At length, when<br>there Comes the Deafening noise | 33. But when<br>the Shout comes |
| 34. That day shall a man<br>flee from his own brother | 34. On the day when a man<br>flee from his brother |
| 35. And from his mother, and his father | 35. And his mother, and his father |
| 36. And from his wife, and his children | 36. And his wife and his children |
| 37. Each one of them, that Day, will have<br>enough concern (of his own)<br>to make him indifferent to the others | 37. Every man that day will have<br>concern enough<br>to make him heedless (of others) |
| 38. Some Faces that Day will be beaming, | 38. On that day faces will be bright as dawn, |
| 39. Laughing, rejoicing. | 39. Laughing, rejoicing at good news; |
| 40. And other faces that Day<br>will be dust stained; | 40. And other faces, on that day,<br>with dust upon them, |
| 41. Blackness will cover them: | 41. Veiled in darkness, |

42. Such will be the Rejecters of Allāh, the doers of inquity.

42. Those are the disbelievers, the wicked.

---

**EXPLANATION:**

80:24-32. There are all kinds of Signs in Nature which point to the Creator. Where does the delicious food that we enjoy so much come from? Skies bring rain, the seed is sown and the Earth breaks open to allow the tiny, delicate seeds to come out (v. 24-26).

These seeds yield all kinds of grasses, wheats, vegetables and fruits. The orchards, gardens and fields grow many different types of food for us and for our animals (v. 27-32).

80:33-37. However, some remain heedless of Allāh's سبحانه وتعالى generosity, and the Day of Judgment is sure to come with a call of *Ṣūr*, the Trumpet (v. 33). That will be a Day of great concern for everyone. Each for himself will be the order of the Day. A brother will not help his own brother, a son will not be concerned about his parents, and a husband will not pay attention to his wife or children (v. 34-36).

80:38-42. On the Day of Judgment, there will be two kinds of faces. The believers will be happy, bright, laughing and rejoicing; and the sinful disbelievers will have sad, sullen, downcast and gloomy faces.

**WE HAVE LEARNED:**

* In Islamic *Da'wah* we must only think of the pleasure of Allāh سبحانه وتعالى and treat everyone equally.
* In our creation, and in the production of food which sustains and supports all life, there is a sign of the Creator for those who care to look.
* The Day of Judgment will surely come, delighting the believers and grieving the disbelievers.

## VOCABULARY

### ٨٠-سُورَةُ عَبَسَ

| | | |
|---|---|---|
| ٢٤-فَلْيَنظُرِ ٱلْإِنسَـٰنُ | *fa-l-yanẓuri-(a)l-'insānu* | Then, let man look |
| إِلَىٰ طَعَامِهِۦ | *'ilā ṭa'āmi-hī* | at his food |
| ٢٥-أَنَّا | *'An-nā* | That We |
| صَبَبْنَا ٱلْمَآءَ | *ṣabab-nā-(a)l-mā'a* | pour forth water |
| صَبًّا | *ṣabban* | in abundance, in heavy shower |

| | | |
|---|---|---|
| ٢٦-ثُمَّ | *Thumma* | Then, |
| شَقَقْنَا ٱلْأَرْضَ | *shaqaq-nā-(a)l-'arḍa* | We split the Earth |
| شَقًّا | *shaqqā(n)* | in parts, in fragments |
| ٢٧-فَأَنْبَتْنَا | *Fa-'anbat-nā* | Then, We caused to grow |
| فِيهَا حَبًّا | *Fī-hā ḥabbā(n)* | therein grain |
| ٢٨-وَعِنَبًا | *Wa-'inaban* | And grapes |
| وَقَضْبًا | *wa-qaḍbā(n)* | and vegetables, fresh vegetation |
| ٢٩-وَزَيْتُونًا | *Wa-zaitūnan* | And olives |
| وَنَخْلًا | *wa-nakhlā(n)* | and dates |
| ٣٠-وَحَدَآئِقَ غُلْبًا | *Wa-ḥadā'iqa ghulbā(n)* | And gardens (of) lofty trees . |
| ٣١-وَفَٰكِهَةً | *Wa-fākihatan* | And fruits |
| وَأَبًّا | *wa-'abbā(n)* | and grass, fodder |
| ٣٢-مَّتَٰعًا لَّكُمْ | *matā'an la-kum* | A provision for you |
| وَلِأَنْعَٰمِكُمْ | *wa-li-'an'āmi-kum* | and for your animals, your cattle. |
| ٣٣-فَإِذَا | *Fa-'idhā* | And when |
| جَآءَتِ ٱلصَّآخَّةُ | *jā'ati-(a)ṣ-Ṣākhkhah(tu)* | comes the Deafening Noise |
| ٣٤-يَوْمَ | *Yawma* | The day |
| يَفِرُّ ٱلْمَرْءُ | *yafirru-(a)l-mar'u* | flees the man |
| مِنْ أَخِيهِ | *min 'akhī-hī* | from his brother |
| ٣٥-وَأُمِّهِ | *Wa-'ummi-hī* | And from his mother |
| وَأَبِيهِ | *wa-'abī-hī* | And his father |

| | | |
|---|---|---|
| ٣٦-وَصَـٰحِبَتِهِۦ | *Wa-ṣāḥibati-hī* | And from his wife, companion |
| وَبَنِيهِ | *wa-banī-hī* | and his children |
| ٣٧-لِكُلِّ ٱمْرِيٍٕ | *Li-kulli-(i)mri'in* | For each one |
| مِّنْهُمْ | *min-hum* | of them |
| يَوْمَئِذٍ شَأْنٌ | *yawma'idhin sha'nun* | on that day (will have) a concern |
| يُغْنِيهِ | *yughnī-hī* | to make him indifferent (to others) |
| ٣٨-وُجُوهٌ يَومَئِذٍ | *Wujūhun yawma'idhin* | (Some) faces on that Day |
| مُّسْفِرَةٌ | *musfiratun* | beaming, bright |
| ٣٩-ضَاحِكَةٌ | *Ḍāḥikatun* | Laughing |
| مُّسْتَبْشِرَةٌ | *mustabshirah(tun)* | rejoicing |
| ٤٠-وَوُجُوهٌ | *Wa-wujūhun* | And (other) faces |
| يَوْمَئِذٍ | *yawma'idhin* | that Day |
| عَلَيْهَا غَبَرَةٌ | *'alai-ha ghabarah(tun)* | on it ( will be ) dust, dust-stained |
| ٤١-تَرْهَقُهَا قَتَرَةٌ | *Tarhaqu-hā qatarah(tun)* | covering them, veiled them (in) darkness |
| ٤٢-أُولَـٰٓئِكَ هُمُ | *'Ulā'ika humu* | Such will be, those are |
| ٱلْكَفَرَةُ ٱلْفَجَرَةُ | *'al-kafaratu-(a)l-fajarah(tu)* | The disbelievers, the wicked |

Lesson 21

سُورَةُ النَّازِعَاتِ

آياتها ٤٦ — ترتيبها ٧٩

# *AN-NĀZI'ĀT, 79:1-26*

## THOSE WHO TEAR OUT / THOSE WHO DRAG FORTH

**Revealed in Makkah**

---

**INTRODUCTION:**

This is an early Makkan *Sūrah*, believed to have been revealed after *Sūrah An-Naba'*, 78.

It deals with the familiar Makkan themes of *Tawḥīd, Risālah* and *'Ākhirah.* It makes reference to the story of Mūsā ﷺ and *Fir'awn*, to demonstrate how arrogance and disbelief lead to self-destruction, even for a mighty ruler such as *Fir'awn* was.

| **TRANSLITERATION:** | **ARABIC TEXT:** |
|---|---|
| *Bismillāhi-(a)r-Raḥmāni-(a)r-Raḥīm(i)* | بِسْمِ اللّٰهِ الرَّحْمٰنِ الرَّحِيْمِ |
| 1. *Wa-(a)n-nāzi'āti gharqā(n)* | -وَالنّٰزِعٰتِ غَرْقًا ۝ |
| 2. *Wa-(a)n-nashiṭāti nashṭā(n)* | -وَّالنّٰشِطٰتِ نَشْطًا ۝ |
| 3. *Wa-(a)s-sābiḥāti sabḥā(n)* | -وَّالسّٰبِحٰتِ سَبْحًا ۝ |
| 4. *Fa-(a)s-sābiqāti sabqā(n)* | -فَالسّٰبِقٰتِ سَبْقًا ۝ |
| 5. *Fa-(a)l-mudabbirāti 'amrā(n)* | -فَالْمُدَبِّرٰتِ اَمْرًا ۝ |
| 6. *Yawma tarjufu-(a)r-rājifah(tu)* | -يَوْمَ تَرْجُفُ الرَّاجِفَةُ ۝ |
| 7. *Tatba'u-ha-(a)r-rādifah(tu)* | -تَتْبَعُهَا الرَّادِفَةُ ۝ |
| 8. *Qulūbun yawma'idhin wājifah(tun)* | -قُلُوْبٌ يَّوْمَئِذٍ وَّاجِفَةٌ ۝ |
| 9. *'Abṣāru-hā khāshi'ah(tun)* | -اَبْصَارُهَا خَاشِعَةٌ ۝ |
| 10. *Yaqūlūna 'a'inna la-mardūdūna fi-(a)l-ḥāfirah(ti)* | -يَقُوْلُوْنَ ءَاِنَّا لَمَرْدُوْدُوْنَ فِى الْحَافِرَةِ ۝ |

| | |
|---|---|
| 11. *'A'idha kunnā 'izāman nakhirah(tan)* | -ءَاِذَا كُنَّا عِظَامًا نَّخِرَةً ۝ |
| 12. *Qālū tilka 'idhan karratun khāsirah(tun)* | -قَالُوْا تِلْكَ اِذًا كَرَّةٌ خَاسِرَةٌ ۝ |
| 13. *Fa-'innamā hiya zajratun wāḥidah(tun)* | -فَاِنَّمَا هِيَ زَجْرَةٌ وَّاحِدَةٌ ۝ |
| 14. *Fa-'idhā hum bi-(a)s-sāhirah(ti)* | -فَاِذَا هُمْ بِالسَّاهِرَةِ ۝ |
| 15. *Hal 'atā-ka ḥadīthu Mūsā* | -هَلْ اَتٰىكَ حَدِيْثُ مُوْسٰى ۝ |
| 16. *'Idh nādā-hu Rabbu-hū bi-(a)l-wādi-(a)l-muqaddasi Ṭuwā* | -اِذْ نَادٰىهُ رَبُّهٗ بِالْوَادِ الْمُقَدَّسِ طُوًى ۝ |
| 17. *'Idhhab 'ilā Fir'awna 'inna-hū ṭaghā* | -اِذْهَبْ اِلٰى فِرْعَوْنَ اِنَّهٗ طَغٰى ۝ |
| 18. *Fa-qul hal-la-ka 'ilā 'an-tazakkā* | -فَقُلْ هَلْ لَّكَ اِلٰٓى اَنْ تَزَكّٰى ۝ |
| 19. *Wa 'ahdiya-ka 'ilā Rabbi-ka fa-takhshā* | -وَاَهْدِيَكَ اِلٰى رَبِّكَ فَتَخْشٰى ۝ |
| 20. *Fa-'arā-hu-(a)l-'āyata-(a)l-kubrā* | -فَاَرٰىهُ الْاٰيَةَ الْكُبْرٰى ۝ |
| 21. *Fa-kadhdhaba wa 'aṣā* | -فَكَذَّبَ وَعَصٰى ۝ |
| 22. *Thumma 'adbara yas'ā* | -ثُمَّ اَدْبَرَ يَسْعٰى ۝ |
| 23. *Fa-ḥashara fa-nādā* | -فَحَشَرَ فَنَادٰى ۝ |
| 24. *Fa-qāla 'anā Rabbu-kumu-(a)l-'a'lā* | -فَقَالَ اَنَا رَبُّكُمُ الْاَعْلٰى ۝ |
| 25. *Fa-'akhadha-hu-(A)llāhu nakāla-(a)l-'ākhirati wa-(a)l-'ūlā* | -فَاَخَذَهُ اللّٰهُ نَكَالَ الْاٰخِرَةِ وَالْاُوْلٰى ۝ |
| 26. *'Inna fī dhālika la 'ibratan li-man yakhshā* | -اِنَّ فِيْ ذٰلِكَ لَعِبْرَةً لِّمَنْ يَّخْشٰى ۝ |

**TRANSLATIONS**:

In the name of Allāh, Most Gracious, Most Merciful.

1. By the (angels) who tear out (the souls of the wicked) with violence;

In the name of Allāh, the Beneficent, the Merciful.

1. By those who drag forth to destruction,

2. By those who gently
draw out (the souls of the blessed)
3. And by those who glide
along (on errands of mercy)
4. Then press forward as in a race,
5. Then arrange to do
(the Commands of their Lord),
6. One Day everything that can be in
commotion will be in violent commotion.
7. Followed by oft-repeated (commotions):
8. Hearts that day will be in agitation;
9. Cast down will be (their owners) eyes.
10. They say (now): "What! Shall have we
indeed be returned to (our) former state?
11. "What! when we shall
have become rotten bones?"
12. They say: "It would, in that case,
be a return with loss!"
13. But Truly, It will be
but a single (compelling) Cry.
14. When, behold, they will be in the
(full) awakening (to judgment),
15. Has the story of
Moses reached you?
16. Behold, Your Lord did call to
him in the sacred valley of *Ṭuwā:*
17. "Go you to Pharaoh, for he has
indeed transgressed all bounds:
18. "And say to him, 'Would you (like)
that you should be purified (from sin)?
19. "And that I guide you to your Lord,
so that you should fear Him?"
20. Then did (Moses) show him
the Great Sign.

2. By the meteors
rushing,
3. By the lone stars
floating,
4. By the angels hastening,
5. And those who
govern the event,
6. On the day when the first
trump resounds
7. And the second follows it,
8. On that day hearts beat painfully
9. While eyes are downcast
10. (Now) they are saying: Shall we
really be restored to our first state
11. Even after we
are crumbled bones?
12. They say: Then that would be
vain proceeding.
13. Surely it will need
but one shout,
14. And lo! they will be
awakened.
15. Has there come to you
the history of Moses?
16. How his Lord call
him in the vale of *Ṭuwā,*
17. (Saying): Go you to Pharaoh-
Lo! he has rebelled-
18. And say (to him): Have you
(will) grow (in grace)?
19. Then I will guide you to your Lord
and you shall fear (Him).
20. And He showed him
the tremendous token

| | |
|---|---|
| 21. But (Pharaoh) rejected it and disobeyed (guidance); | 21. But he denied and disobeyed, |
| 22. Further, he turned his back, striving hard (against Allāh). | 22. Then turned he away in haste, |
| 23. Then he collected (his men) and made a proclamation, | 23. Then gathered he and summoned |
| 24. Saying, "I am your Lord, Most High." | 24. And proclaimed: "I (Pharaoh) am your Lord the Highest." |
| 25. But Allāh did punish him, (and made an) example of him, in the Hereafter, as in this life. | 25. So Allāh seized him (and made him) an example for the after life and for the former |
| 26. Truly in this is an instructive warning for whosoever fears (Allāh). | 26. Lo! herein is indeed a lesson for him who fears. |

---

**EXPLANATION**:

79:1-5. The first five verses are oaths of Allāh ﷻ, to verify the coming of the Day of Judgment. These are subject to different interpretations. Yūsuf 'Ali and Pickthal differ in their understanding of these verses. We found Yūsuf 'Ali to be closer to traditional understanding.

The oath of the Angels refers to their various duties as commanded by Allāh ﷻ. Angels take out the souls of disbelievers harshly, and the souls of the believers are removed gently (v.1-2). The souls glide along, going ahead, as if in a race, eager to fulfill the commands of Allāh ﷻ (v. 3- 5).

79:6-9. On the Day of Judgment, there will be two violent commotions. The first will destroy everything, and the second will bring everything to life. The commotion may be due to the blowing of the *Ṣūr,* the Trumpet (v. 6-7).

Some hearts on that Day will beat fast, with agitation, and their eyes will be downcast in fear (v.8-9). Though everyone will be fearful on that unusual Day, according to some Traditions of Rasūlullāh ﷺ, the believers will receive reassurance from Allāh ﷻ, and will be happy.

79:10-14. The *Kuffār* did not believe in the Resurrection and the afterlife (v. 10). They demanded to know how crushed and rotted bones could be brought back to life. They were so firm in their disbelief of the *'Ākhirah* that they mocked its occurence by saying that it would be a real loss for them if they did return (v. 11-12).

Allāh „ Who created the world and the Angels and mankind, could certainly re-create all of these things without difficulty. One Command will awaken us from death (v. 13-14).

79:15-20. The story of Mūsā and his confrontation with *Fir'awn* is recalled here. Allāh called Mūsā in the valley of *Ṭuwā* in Sinai.

Mūsā was returning from his exile in Midian, to where he had fled, fearing reprisal from *Fir'awn.* There he spent some time and married the two daughters of the Prophet Shu'aib. There was a fire visible some distance away. He went to fetch the fire. He heard the call from Allāh to remove his shoes as a show of respect. In fact, it was not fire that he saw but rather, the Burning Bush, a sign of Allāh's Light. There, Mūsā received his prophetic mission to go to *Fir'awn* who had transgressed the Divine Command (v. 15-17).

*Fir'awn*, the Egyptian ruler, was worshipped as a god by his subjects. The Egyptians also worshipped many other gods and goddesses. Mūsā was asked to invite *Fir'awn* to purify himself from sinful ideas and false arrogance. *Fir'awn* was commanded to give up his pretensions of being a god and to return to the worship of the One True God (v.18-19). Mūsā was given several miracles, the *Mu'jizāt,* to convince *Fir'awn* and his courtiers. These included a hand that shone as he brought it out of his armpit, and a staff that would turn into a snake when he threw it to the ground.

79:21-24. However, despite the clear message and accompanying miracles, *Fir'awn* was not convinced. He rejected the truth and disobeyed Allāh's Commandment. In defiance of Mūsā's call, he declared himself as the supreme lord before his people.

79:25-26. The arrogance of *Fir'awn* did not help him to succeed. Allāh punished him by drowning him in the Red Sea (v. 25). He has been made an example for the God-fearing and we are to learn a lesson from his arrogant rule and humiliating death.

**WE HAVE LEARNED:**

* The blowing of the *Ṣūr* will signal the beginning of the Day of Judgment.
* Mūsā was sent to *Fir'awn* to invite him to Allāh's *Dīn, Al-Islām.*
* *Fir'awn* declined to accept in arrogance and was destroyed because of his pride.

## VOCABULARY

### ٧٩-سُورَةُ ٱلنَّازِعَاتِ

| | | |
|---|---|---|
| ١-وَٱلنَّٰزِعَٰتِ | *Wa-(a)n-nāzi'āt(i)* | By those (angels) who tear out, those who drag forth ( the souls of the wicked) |
| غَرْقًا | *gharqā(n)* | with violence, with difficulty |
| ٢-وَٱلنَّٰشِطَٰتِ | *Wa-(a)n-nāshiṭāt(i)* | And by those (angels) who draw out gently ( the souls of the blessed) |
| نَشْطًا | *nashṭā(n)* | gently, easily |
| ٣-وَٱلسَّٰبِحَٰتِ سَبْحًا | *Wa-(a)s-sābiḥāti sabḥā(n)* | And by those (angels) who glide along (on errands of mercy) |
| ٤-فَٱلسَّٰبِقَٰتِ سَبْقًا | *Fa-(a)s-sābiqāti sabqā(n)* | By those (angels) who press forward as in a race |
| ٥-فَٱلْمُدَبِّرَاتِ | *Fa-(a)l-mudabbirāti* | then arrange to do |
| أمْراً | *'amrā(n)* | the orders ( of their Lord) |
| ٦-يَوْمَ | *Yawma* | ( That ) Day |
| تَرْجُفُ ٱلرَّاجِفَةُ | *tarjufu-(a)r-rājifah(tu)* | when there will be great commotion |
| ٧-تَتْبَعُهَا | *Tatba'u-hā* | It is followed with |
| الرَّادِفَةُ | *'ar-rādifah(tu)* | a second one |
| ٨-قُلُوبٌ | *Qulūb(un)* | Hearts |
| يَوْمَئِذٍ وَاجِفَةٌ | *yawma'idhin wājifah(tun)* | that day will be in pain, in agitation |
| ٩-أَبْصَٰرُهَا | *'Abṣāru-hā* | Their owners' eyes |
| خَٰشِعَةٌ | *khāshi'ah(tun)* | will be downcast |
| ١٠-يَقُولُونَ | *Yaqūlūna* | They say |
| أَءِنَّا لَمَرْدُودُونَ | *'a-'innā la-mardūdūna* | shall we indeed be returned |
| فِي ٱلْحَافِرَةِ | *fi-(a)l-ḥāfirah(ti)* | to our first state ( of life ) |

| | | |
|---|---|---|
| ١١-أَءِذَا كُنَّا | *'A-'i<u>dh</u>ā-kunnā* | Even after we are |
| عِظَـٰمًا نَّخِرَةً | *'iẓāman na<u>kh</u>irah(tan)* | bones rotten, crumbled |
| ١٢-قَالُوا | *Qālū* | They say |
| تِلْكَ إِذًا | *tilka 'i<u>dh</u>an* | that then |
| كَرَّةٌ خَاسِرَةٌ | *karratun <u>kh</u>āsirah(tun)* | will be a return with loss |
| ١٣-فَإِنَّمَا هِيَ | *Fa-'innamā hiya* | But it will be |
| زَجْرَةٌ وَاحِدَةٌ | *zajratun wāḥidah(tun)* | one cry, one shout |
| ١٤-فَإِذَا هُم | *Fa-'i<u>dh</u>a hum* | And they will (be) |
| بِٱلسَّاهِرَةِ | *bi-(a)s-sāhirah(ti)* | awakened, (brought out to the open) |
| ١٥-هَلْ أَتَـٰكَ | *Hal 'atā-ka* | Has it reached you |
| حَدِيثُ مُوسَىٰ | *ḥadī<u>th</u>u Mūsā* | the story of Moses, |
| ١٦-إِذْ نَادَىٰهُ | *'I<u>dh</u> nādā-hu* | When He did call to him |
| رَبُّهُ | *Rabbu-hū* | His Lord |
| بِٱلْوَادِ ٱلْمُقَدَّسِ | *bi-(a)l-wādi-l-muqaddasi* | In the sacred valley |
| طُوًى | *Ṭuwā(n)* | of *Ṭuwa* |
| ١٧-اذْهَبْ | *'i<u>dh</u>hab* | You go |
| إِلَىٰ فِرْعَوْنَ | *'ilā Fir'awna* | to Pharaoh |
| إِنَّهُ طَغَىٰ | *'inna-hū ṭa<u>gh</u>ā* | indeed he has transgressed the bounds |
| ١٨-فَقُلْ | *Fa-qul* | And tell (him) |
| هَل لَّكَ | *hal la-ka* | Have you desire |
| إِلَىٰ أَنْ تَزَكَّىٰ | *'ila 'an tazakkā* | that you be purified, you grow (in grace) |
| ١٩-وَأَهْدِيَكَ | *Wa-'ahdiya-ka* | And I guide you |
| إِلَىٰ رَبِّكَ | *'ilā Rabbi-ka* | to your Lord |

| | | |
|---|---|---|
| فَتَخْشَىٰ | fa-takhshā | so, you shall fear (Him) |
| ٢٠-فَأَرَاهُ | Fa-'arā-hu | Then he (Mūsā) showed him |
| اَلْأَيَةَ ٱلْكُبْرَىٰ | 'al-'āyat-(a)l-kubrā | the Great Sign, the Tremendous Token |
| ٢١-فَكَذَّبَ وَعَصَىٰ | Fa-kadhdhaba wa-'aṣā | But he denied and disobeyed |
| ٢٢-ثُمَّ أَدْبَرَ | Thumma 'adbara | Then he turned away |
| يَسْعَىٰ | yas'ā | striving hard ( against Allah) |
| ٢٣-فَحَشَرَ | Fa-ḥashara | Then he gathered (his men) |
| فَنَادَىٰ | Fa-nādā | and declared |
| ٢٤-فَقَالَ أَنَا | Fa-qāla 'anā | And said: I am |
| رَبُّكُمُ ٱلْأَعْلَىٰ | rabbu-kum-(a)l-'a'lā | your lord, most high |
| ٢٥-فَأَخَذَهُ ٱللَّهُ | Fa-'akhadha-hu-(A)llāhu | Then, Allah punished him, seized him |
| نَكَالَ | nakāla | (made an) example |
| اَلْأَخِرَةِ وَٱلْأُولَىٰ | 'al-'ākhirati wa-(a)l-'ūlā | for the Hereafter and in this life |
| ٢٦-إِنَّ فِى ذَلِكَ | 'Inna fī dhālika | Indeed in this is |
| لَعِبْرَةً | la-'ibratan | a lesson |
| لِمَنْ يَخْشَىٰ | li-man yakhshā | for whosoever fears |

*Lesson 22*

# *AN-NĀZI‘ĀT, 79:27-46*

## THOSE WHO TEAR OUT / THOSE WHO DRAG FORTH

**Revealed in Makkah**

---

| **TRANSLITERATION:** | **ARABIC TEXT:** |
|---|---|
| 27. *’A ’antum ’ashaddu khalqan ’ami-(a)s-samā’u banā-hā* | -ءَأَنْتُمْ أَشَدُّ خَلْقًا أَمِ السَّمَاءُ بَنٰهَا ○ |
| 28. *Rafa‘a samka-hā fa-sawwā-hā* | -رَفَعَ سَمْكَهَا فَسَوّٰهَا ○ |
| 29. *Wa ’aghṭasha laila-hā wa ’akhraja ḍuḥā-hā* | -وَأَغْطَشَ لَيْلَهَا وَأَخْرَجَ ضُحٰهَا ○ |
| 30. *Wa-(a)l-’arḍa ba‘da dhālika daḥā-hā* | -وَالْأَرْضَ بَعْدَ ذٰلِكَ دَحٰهَا ○ |
| 31. *’Akhraja min-hā mā’a-hā wa mar‘ā-hā* | -أَخْرَجَ مِنْهَا مَاءَهَا وَمَرْعٰهَا ○ |
| 32. *Wa-(a)l-jibāla ’arsā-hā* | -وَالْجِبَالَ أَرْسٰهَا ○ |
| 33. *Matā‘an la-kum wa li-an‘āmi-kum* | -مَتَاعًا لَّكُمْ وَلِأَنْعَامِكُمْ ○ |
| 34. *Fa-’idhā jā‘ati-(a)ṭ-ṭāmmatu-(a)l-kubrā* | -فَإِذَا جَاءَتِ الطَّامَّةُ الْكُبْرٰى ○ |
| 35. *Yawma yatadhakkaru-(a)l-’insānu mā-sa‘ā* | -يَوْمَ يَتَذَكَّرُ الْإِنْسَانُ مَا سَعٰى ○ |
| 36. *Wa burrizati-(a)l-jaḥīmu li-man yarā* | -وَبُرِّزَتِ الْجَحِيمُ لِمَنْ يَّرٰى ○ |
| 37. *Fa-’ammā man ṭaghā* | -فَأَمَّا مَنْ طَغٰى ○ |
| 38. *Wa ’āthara-(a)l-ḥayāta-(a)d-dunyā* | -وَاٰثَرَ الْحَيٰوةَ الدُّنْيَا ○ |
| 39. *Fa-’inna-(a)l-jaḥīma hiya-(a)l-ma’wā* | -فَإِنَّ الْجَحِيمَ هِيَ الْمَأْوٰى ○ |
| 40. *Wa ’ammā man khāfa maqāma Rabbi-hī* | -وَأَمَّا مَنْ خَافَ مَقَامَ رَبِّهِ |
| *wa nahan-nafsa ‘ani-(a)l-hawā* | وَنَهَى النَّفْسَ عَنِ الْهَوٰى ○ |

41. *Fa-'inna-(a)l-Jannata hiya-(a)l-ma'wā* — فَإِنَّ الْجَنَّةَ هِيَ الْمَأْوَىٰ ۝

42. *Yas'alūna-ka 'ani-(a)s-sā'ati 'ayyāna mursā-hā* — يَسْـَٔلُونَكَ عَنِ السَّاعَةِ أَيَّانَ مُرْسَاهَا ۝

43. *Fī-mā 'anta min dhikrā-hā* — فِيمَ أَنتَ مِن ذِكْرَاهَا ۝

44. *'Ilā Rabbi-ka muntahā-hā* — إِلَىٰ رَبِّكَ مُنتَهَاهَا ۝

45. *'Innamā 'anta mundhiru man yakhshā-hā* — إِنَّمَا أَنتَ مُنذِرُ مَن يَخْشَاهَا ۝

46. *Ka-'annan-hum yawma yarawna-hā lam-yalbathū 'illā* — كَأَنَّهُمْ يَوْمَ يَرَوْنَهَا لَمْ يَلْبَثُوا إِلَّا

*'ashīyyatan 'aw ḍuḥā-hā* — عَشِيَّةً أَوْ ضُحَاهَا ۝

**TRANSLATIONS:**

| | |
|---|---|
| 27. What! Are you the more difficult to create or the heaven (above)? (Allāh) has constructed it: | 27. Are you the harder to create, or is the heaven that He built? |
| 28. On high has He raised its canopy, and He has given it order and perfection. | 28. He raised the height thereof and ordered it; |
| 29. Its night does He endow with darkness, and its splendour does He bring out (with light). | 29. And He made dark the night thereof, and He brought forth the morn thereof. |
| 30. And the earth, moreover, has he extended (to a wide expanse); | 30. And after that He spread the earth, |
| 31. He draws out from it its moisture and its pasture; | 31. And produced therefrom the water thereof and the pasture thereof, |
| 32. And the mountains has He firmly fixed; | 32. And He made fast the hills, |
| 33. For use and convenience to you and your cattle. | 33. A provision for you and for your cattle. |
| 34. Therefore, when there comes the great, overwhelming (Event), | 34. But when the great disaster comes, |
| 35. The Day when Man shall remember (all) that he strove for, | 35. The day when man will call to mind his (whole) endeavour, |
| 36. And Hell-Fire shall be placed in full view for all to see, | 36. And hell will stand forth visible to him who sees, |
| 37. Then for such as had transgressed all bounds, | 37. Then, as for him who rebelled |

38. And had preferred the life of this world,
39. The abode will be Hell-Fire;
40. And for such as had entertained the fear of standing before their Lord's (tribunal) and had restrained (their) soul from lower Desires.
41. Their Abode will be the Garden.
42. They ask you about the hour,
Where will be its appointed time?
43. Why are you (concerned)
with its declaration?
44. With your Lord is the
Limit fixed for it.
45. You are but a Warner
for such as fear it.
46. The Day they see it (it will be) as if they
had tarried but a single evening,
or (at most till) the following morn!

38. And chose the life of the world,
39. Lo! hell will be his home.
40. But as for him who feared to
stand before his Lord and
restrained his soul from lust,
41. Lo! the Garden will be his home.
42. They ask you of the Hour:
when will it come to port?
43. Why (ask they)? What have you
to tell thereof?
44. To your Lord belonges
(knowledge of) the term thereof.
45. You are but a warner to him
who fears it.
46. On the day when they behold it,
it will be as if they had but tarried for an
evening or the morn thereof.

---

**EXPLANATION**:

79:27-33. Allāh سبحانه وتعالى is the Creator of human beings, He will cause them to die and recreate them on the Day of Judgment. For Allāh سبحانه وتعالى, neither creation nor recreation is difficult. Human beings are a small part of His cosmic creation. Allāh سبحانه وتعالى, therefore asks a rhetorical question: "What is more difficult, to make human beings or to make the whole cosmic order? (v. 27)."

The duly proportioned Heaven (v. 27-28); the system of day and night (v. 29); the wide, expanding Earth, which provides water and pasture to sustain life (v. 30-31); the firmly established high-rising mountains (v. 32) are all provisions for man and his animals (v. 33), and all testify to the Wisdom and Power of Allāh سبحانه وتعالى.

79:34-36. All the Power of Allāh سبحانه وتعالى is enough proof of the truth of His promise of the Day of Judgment. That overwhelming event is sure to come (v. 34). On that Day, man will know what actions were done by him in this world (v. 35). The Fire of Hell will be in full view of the evil-doers (v. 36).

79.37-39. The Day of Judgment is a Day of Decision for the evil-doers and for the believers. For those who did not accept Allāh's Laws, transgressed His commands and enjoyed the life of this world; preferring it over the life of the Hereafter; their place will be in the Fire of Hell.

79:40-41. The people who believed that they would one day stand before Allāh ﷻ, and accordingly followed Allāh's ﷻ commands, will be rewarded with the *Jannah*, as their eternal home.

79:42-46. The *Kuffār* mockingly asked Rasūlullāh ﷺ about the time of the Hour of Judgment. Only Allāh ﷻ has exact knowledge of that, Rasūlullāh ﷺ did not have to worry about such questions, and to Him is the final return (v. 42-44).

Rasūlullāh ﷺ was sent only as a warner, for those who cared to listen to his Message and adopt a life of faith and righteous deeds. He did not force people to accept the Message or try to convince them through argument (v. 45).

People may deny the truth of the Hereafter now, but they will soon see that Day for themselves. Then, they will wake up from death, thinking that they were waking from an evening nap or morning sleep (v. 46).

**WE HAVE LEARNED:**

* Allāh ﷻ is the Creator of not only human beings but of the entire cosmic order.
* All the creations of Allāh ﷻ are for the benefit of human beings.
* Human beings must be thankful to Allāh ﷻ and prepare for the Hereafter.

## VOCABULARY II

### ٧٩-سُورَةُ النَّازِعَاتِ

| | | |
|---|---|---|
| ٢٧-ءَأَنتُمْ | *'A-'antum* | Are you |
| أَشَدُّ خَلْقًا | *'ashaddu khalqan* | harder to create |
| أَمِ السَّمَآءُ | *'ami-(a)s-samā'u* | or the sky, or the heaven |
| بَنَـٰهَا | *banā-hā* | He built it |
| ٢٨-رَفَعَ سَمْكَهَا | *Rafa'a samka-hā* | Raised its height |
| فَسَوَّاهَا | *Fa-sawwā-hā* | then ordered it, gave it perfection |
| ٢٩-وَأَغْطَشَ لَيْلَهَا | *Wa-'aghtasha laila-hā* | He made dark its night |

| | | |
|---|---|---|
| وَأَخْرَجَ ضُحَـٰهَا | *wa-'akhraja ḍuḥā-hā* | and brings out its morning |
| ٣٠-وَٱلأَرْضَ | *Wa-(a)l-'arḍa* | And the Earth |
| بَعْدَ ذَٰلِكَ | *ba'da dhālika* | moreover, after that |
| دَحَـٰهَآ | *daḥā-hā* | He extended, spread |
| ٣١-أَخْرَجَ مِنْهَا | *'akhraja min-hā* | brought out from it, produced |
| مَآءَهَا | *mā'a-hā* | its water |
| وَمَرْعَـٰهَا | *wa-mar'ā-hā* | and its pasture |
| ٣٢-وَٱلْجِبَالَ | *Wa-(a)l-jibāla* | And the mountains |
| أَرْسَـٰهَا | *'arsā-hā* | He made them firm |
| ٣٣-مَتَـٰعًا لَّكُمْ | *matā'an la-kum* | A provision for you |
| وَلِأَنْعَـٰمِكُمْ | *wa-li-'an'āmi-kum* | And for your animals |
| ٣٤-فَإِذَا جَآءَتِ | *Fa-'idhā jā'at(i)* | Therefore when there comes |
| ٱلطَّآمَّةُ ٱلْكُبْرَىٰ | *'aṭ-ṭāmmatu-(a)l-kubrā* | great disaster, the great event |
| ٣٥-يَوْمَ | *Yawma* | The day |
| يَتَذَكَّرُ ٱلإِنْسَـٰنُ | *yatadhakkaru -(a)l-'insānu* | remembers the man |
| مَا سَعَىٰ | *mā sa'ā* | what he strove for |
| ٣٦-وَبُرِّزَتِ ٱلْجَحِيمُ | *wa-burrizati-(a)l-Jaḥīmu* | is made visible the Hell-Fire |
| لِمَنْ يَرَىٰ | *li-man yarā* | for one who sees |
| ٣٧-فَأَمَّا | *Fa-'ammā* | Then as for |
| مَنْ طَغَىٰ | *man ṭaghā* | one who rebelled |
| ٣٨-وَءَاثَرَ | *Wa-'āthara* | And prefers |
| ٱلْحَيَوٰةَ ٱلدُّنْيَا | *'al-ḥayāta-(a)d-dunyā* | the life of this world |
| ٣٩- فَإِنَّ ٱلْجَحِيمَ | *Fa-'inna-(a)l-Jaḥīma* | Surely, the Hell-Fire |

| | | |
|---|---|---|
| هِيَ ٱلْمَأْوَىٰ | *hiya-(a)l-ma'wā* | will be the abode |
| ٤٠-وَأَمَّا | *Wa-'ammā* | As for |
| مَنْ خَافَ | *man khāfa* | one who fears |
| مَقَامَ رَبِّهِ | *maqāma Rabbi-hī* | to standing before his Lord |
| وَنَهَى ٱلنَّفْسَ | *wa-naha-(a)n-nafsa* | and restrained the soul |
| عَنِ ٱلْهَوَىٰ | *'ani-(a)l-hawā* | from the desire, lust |
| ٤١-فَإِنَّ ٱلْجَنَّةَ | *Fa-'inna-(a)l-Jannata* | Indeed, the *Jannah* |
| هِيَ ٱلْمَأْوَىٰ | *hiya-(a)l-ma'wā* | will be the abode |
| ٤٢-يَسْئَلُونَكَ | *Yas'alūna-ka* | They ask you |
| عَنِ ٱلسَّاعَةِ | *'ani-(a)s-Sā'ati* | about the hour |
| أَيَّانَ مُرْسَـٰهَا | *'ayyāna mursā-hā* | when will be its appointed time |
| ٤٣-فِيمَ أَنْتَ | *Fī-ma 'anta* | Why are you concerned |
| مِنْ ذِكْرَاهَآ | *min dhikrā-hā* | with the declaration |
| ٤٤-إِلَىٰ رَبِّكَ | *'Ilā Rabbi-ka* | With your Lord |
| مُنتَهَـٰهَآ | *muntahā-hā* | (is) its final end |
| ٤٥-إِنَّمَآ أَنْتَ | *'innamā 'anta* | Indeed you are |
| مُنْذِرُ | *mundhiru* | a warner |
| مَنْ يَخْشَـٰهَا | *man yakhshā-hā* | who fears it |
| ٤٦-كَأَنَّهُمْ | *Ka-'anna-hum* | It will be as if |
| يَوْمَ يَرَوْنَهَا | *yawma yarawna-hā* | the day they see it |
| لَمْ يَلْبَثُوٓا | *lam yalbathū* | they did not live |
| إِلاَّ عَشِيَّةً | *'illa 'ashiyyatan* | except an evening |
| أَوْ ضُحَـٰهَا | *'aw duhā-hā* | or a morning |

*Lesson 23*

سُورَةُ النَّبَإِ

# *AN-NABA', 78:1-25*

## THE (GREAT) NEWS / THE TIDING

**Revealed in Makkah**

---

**INTRODUCTION:**

This is one of the earlier Makkan *Suwar*. Like all other *Suwar* from this period, it deals with three major concepts: *Tawḥīd,* Oneness of God, the *Risālah,* the finality of Rasūlullāh's mission, and the *'Ākhirah,* the Hereafter.

The *Kuffār* recognized many gods, and they accepted *Shirk* as a way of life. They were prepared to recognize the integrity and honesty of Rasūlullāh ﷺ, but were not prepared to accept his Message of *Tawḥīd.* Their greatest difficulty was in accepting the concept of the *'Ākhirah,* the Day of Judgment. They were a proud and independent people, and were quite unprepared to accept any moral code for themselves or any responsibility for their actions.

This *Sūrah* proclaims the certainty of the Day of Judgment, and gives evidence of the Unity of Allāh سبحانه وتعالى, through the mention of some natural phenomena. It also warns of the consequences in the *'Ākhirah* for non-believers and offers promises of reward for the believers.

| **TRANSLITERATION:** | **ARABIC TEXT:** |
|---|---|
| *Bismillāhi-(a)r-Raḥmāni-(a)r-Raḥīm(i)* | بِسْمِ اللَّهِ الرَّحْمَٰنِ الرَّحِيمِ |
| 1. *'Amma yatasā'alūn(a)* | عَمَّ يَتَسَاءَلُونَ ۝ -١ |
| 2. *'Ani-(a)n-naba'i-(a)l-'aẓīm(i)* | عَنِ النَّبَإِ الْعَظِيمِ ۝ -٢ |
| 3. *'Alladhī hum fī-hi mukhtalifūn(a)* | الَّذِي هُمْ فِيهِ مُخْتَلِفُونَ ۝ -٣ |
| 4. *Kallā sa-ya'lamūn(a)* | كَلَّا سَيَعْلَمُونَ ۝ -٤ |
| 5. *Thumma kallā sa-ya'lamūn(a)* | ثُمَّ كَلَّا سَيَعْلَمُونَ ۝ -٥ |
| 6. *'A-lam naj'ali-(a)l-'arḍa mihādā(n)* | أَلَمْ نَجْعَلِ الْأَرْضَ مِهَادًا ۝ |

| | | |
|---|---|---|
| 7. | Wa-(a)l-jibāla ’awtadā(n) | وَّالْجِبَالَ أَوْتَادًا ○ |
| 8. | Wa khalaq-nā-kum ’azwājā(n) | -وَّخَلَقْنَٰكُمْ أَزْوَٰجًا ○ |
| 9. | Wa ja‘al-nā nawma-kum subātā(n) | -وَّجَعَلْنَا نَوْمَكُمْ سُبَاتًا ○ |
| 10. | Wa ja‘al-na-(a)l-laila libāsā(n) | -وَّجَعَلْنَا الَّيْلَ لِبَاسًا ○ |
| 11. | Wa ja‘al-na-(a)n-nahāra ma‘āshā(n) | -وَّجَعَلْنَا النَّهَارَ مَعَاشًا ○ |
| 12. | Wa banai-nā fawqa-kum sab‘an shidādā(n) | -وَبَنَيْنَا فَوْقَكُمْ سَبْعًا شِدَادًا ○ |
| 13. | Wa ja‘al-nā sirājan wahhājā(n) | -وَّجَعَلْنَا سِرَاجًا وَّهَّاجًا ○ |
| 14. | Wa ’anzal-nā mina-(a)l-mu‘ṣirāti mā’an thājjājā(n) | -وَّأَنْزَلْنَا مِنَ الْمُعْصِرَٰتِ مَآءً ثَجَّاجًا ○ |
| 15. | Li-nukhrija bi-hī ḥabban wa nabātā(n) | -لِّنُخْرِجَ بِهِۦ حَبًّا وَّنَبَاتًا ○ |
| 16. | Wa jannātin ’alfāfā(n) | -وَّجَنَّٰتٍ أَلْفَافًا ○ |
| 17. | ’Inna yawma-(a)l-faṣli kāna mīqātā(n) | -إِنَّ يَوْمَ الْفَصْلِ كَانَ مِيقَٰتًا ○ |
| 18. | Yawma yunfakhu fī-(a)ṣ-ṣūri fa-ta’tūna ’afwājā(n) | -يَوْمَ يُنْفَخُ فِي الصُّورِ فَتَأْتُونَ أَفْوَاجًا ○ |
| 19. | Wa futiḥati-(a)s-samā’u fa-kānat ’abwābā(n) | -وَّفُتِحَتِ السَّمَآءُ فَكَانَتْ أَبْوَٰبًا ○ |
| 20. | Wa suyyirati-(a)l-jibālu fa-kānat sarābā(n) | -وَّسُيِّرَتِ الْجِبَالُ فَكَانَتْ سَرَابًا ○ |
| 21. | ’Inna jahannama kānat mirṣādā(n) | -إِنَّ جَهَنَّمَ كَانَتْ مِرْصَادًا ○ |
| 22. | Li-(a)ṭ-ṭāghīna ma’ābā(n) | -لِّلطَّٰغِينَ مَـَٔابًا ○ |
| 23. | Lābithīna fī-hā ’aḥqābā(n) | -لَّٰبِثِينَ فِيهَآ أَحْقَابًا ○ |
| 24. | Lā-yadhūqūna fī-hā bardan wa lā sharābā(n) | -لَّا يَذُوقُونَ فِيهَا بَرْدًا وَّلَا شَرَابًا ○ |
| 25. | ’Illā ḥamīman wa ghassāqā(n) | -إِلَّا حَمِيمًا وَّغَسَّاقًا ○ |

**TRANSLATIONS:**

In the name of Allāh, Most Gracious,
Most Merciful.

1. Concerning what are they disputing?
2. Concerning the Great News,
3. About which they cannot agree.
4. Truly, they shall soon (come to) know!
5. Truly, truly they shall soon (come to) know!
6. Have We not made the earth as a wide expanse,
7. And the mountains as pegs?
8. And (have We not) created you in pairs,
9. And made your sleep for rest,
10. And made the night as a covering
11. And made the day as means of subsistence
12. And (have We not) built over you the seven firmaments,
13. And placed (in it) Light of Splendour?
14. And do We not send down from the clouds water in abundance
15. That We may produce with it corn and vegetables,
16. And gardens of luxurious growth?
17. Truly the Day of Sorting Out is a thing appointed,
18. The Day that the Trumpet shall be sounded, and you shall come forth in crowds;
19. And the Heaven shall be opened as if there were doors,
20. And the mountains shall vanish, as if they were a mirage.
21. Truly Hell is as a place of ambush,

In the name of Allāh, the Beneficent,
the Merciful.

1. Whereof do they question one another?
2. (It is) of the awful tidings,
3. Concerning which they are in disagreement.
4. Nay, but they will come to know!
5. Nay, again, but they will come to know!
6. Have We not made the earth an expanse,
7. And the high hills bulkwarks?
8. And We have created you pairs,
9. And have appointed your sleep for repose,
10. And have appointed the night as cloak,
11. And have appointed the day for livelihood.
12. And We have built above you seven strong (heavens),
13. And have appointed a dazzling lamp,
14. And have sent down from the rainy clouds abundant water,
15. Thereby to produce grain and plant,
16. And gardens of thick foliage.
17. Lo! the Day of Decision is a fixed time,
18. A day when the trumpet is blown, and you come in multitudes,
19. And the heaven is opened and become as gates.
20. And the hills are set in motion and become mirage
21. Lo! hell lurks in ambush,

22. For the transgressors a place of destination:
23. They will dwell in it ages.
24. Nothing cool shall they taste in it, nor any drink.
25. Except a boiling fluid and a fluid dark, murky, intensely cold,

22. A home for the rebellious.
23. They will abide therein for ages.
24. Therein taste they neither coolness nor (any) drink
25. Save boiling water and a paralysing cold:

---

**EXPLANATION:**

78:1-5. The Qur'ān informed the *Kuffār* about the certainty of the Day of Judgment. Most of the *Kuffār* did not believe that they could be reborn after becoming dust and ashes. Some of them did believe in some form of life after death, but they were not clear about its nature. The Qur'ānic Revelation touched off this controversy. The *Kuffār* were arguing about the *An-Naba'i-(a)l-'Azīm*, the Great News of the certainty of the Day of Judgment.

The Day of Judgment is a certainty and everyone will witness it.

78:6-16. These verses hold descriptions of Nature to emphasize the Power of Creativity of Allāh . They serve to show His Greatness and His unquestionable Ability to recreate mankind on the Day of Judgment.

The Earth has been spread out in a wide expanse for our use. The mountains stand as solid pegs in the ground (v. 6-7).

Allāh has fashioned us and His other creations in pairs (v. 8). Each member of these pairs is associated with the other in many obvious and mysterious ways. Human and animal pairs account for the phenomenon of creativity and continuity.

Allāh created night for rest and made it dark, as a covering, to help us relax. He made the day bright so that we may seek our livelihood through struggle and work (v. 9-11).

The seven Heavens are firmly established. We do not know their nature but they are a part of Allāh's cosmic plan.

The sun shines like a blazing lamp providing warmth and light. The whole process of growth, life, vegetation and rainfall is dependent on the sun. (v.13). The clouds send down rain, which supports both the human life and the vegetation (v.14).

All of these things are Signs of Allāh's Power and Majesty. These are, in themselves, proof that He will recreate human beings and establish the Day of *Qiyāmah.*

78:17-20. The Day of Sorting is the Day of Judgment, when good and bad will be sorted for Judgment. This Day is a certainty (v. 17). On that Day, Angel *'Isrāfīl* ﷺ will sound the Trumpet to herald the beginning of the Day of Judgment (v. 18).

There will be a terrible convulsion, during which the boundaries between Heaven and Earth will disappear. Human beings will be able to see for themselves the mysteries of Heaven (v. 19).

The convulsion will cause mountains to fly and disappear (v. 19). Hell will eagerly await evil persons to be thrown into it, and those sinners who defied Allāh's commands will find therein a final destination (v. 21-23).

78:24-25. The drink of Hell will not be cool and sweet water, but will be a dark and murky drink, boiling and so cold that it will be impossible to drink.

**WE HAVE LEARNED:**

* No one knows the time of the Day of Judgment, but its certainty no one should deny.
* On that Day with the sound of the *Ṣūr* heavens will open up and a new world order would appear.
* Those who denied this day and did not prepare for it will receive severe punishment.

## VOCABULARY

### ٧٨- سُورَةُ ٱلنَّبَإِ

| | | |
|---|---|---|
| ١-عَمَّ يَتَسَآءَلُونَ | *'Amma yatasā'alūn(a)* | Concerning what do they question |
| ٢-عَنِ ٱلنَّبَإِ ٱلْعَظِيمِ | *'Ani-(a)n-naba'i-(a)l-'aẓīm(i)* | Concerning great news |
| ٣- ٱلَّذِى هُمْ | *'Alladhī hum* | That they |
| فِيهِ مُخْتَلِفُونَ | *fī-hī mukhtalifūn(a)* | about it disagree |
| ٤-كَلَّا سَيَعْلَمُونَ | *Kallā sa-ya'lamūn(a)* | Verily, nay, they will soon know |
| ٥-ثُمَّ كَلَّا | *Thumma kallā* | Again , verily |
| سَيَعْلَمُونَ | *sa-ya'lamūn(a)* | they will soon know |
| ٦-أَلَمْ نَجْعَلِ | *'Alam naj'al(i)* | Have We not made |
| ٱلأَرْضَ مِهَٰدًا | *'al'-arḍa mihādā(n)* | the Earth as a wide expanse |
| ٧-وَٱلْجِبَالَ أَوْتَادًا | *Wa-(a)l-jibāla 'awtādā(n)* | And the mountain as pegs |
| ٨-وَخَلَقْنَٰكُمْ | *Wa-khalaq-Nā-kum* | And We created you |
| أَزْوَٰجًا | *'azwājā(n)* | in pairs |

| | | |
|---|---|---|
| ٩-وَجَعَلْنَا | *Wa-ja'al-nā* | And We made |
| نَوْمَكُمْ سُبَاتًا | *nawma-kum subātā(n)* | your sleep a repose |
| ١٠-وَجَعَلْنَا | *Wa-ja'al-nā* | And We made |
| اَلَّيْلَ لِبَاسًا | *'al-laila libāsā(n)* | The night a covering |
| ١١-وَجَعَلْنَا | *Wa-ja'al-nā* | And We made |
| اَلنَّهارَ مَعَاشًا | *'an-nahāra ma'āshā(n)* | the day for livelihood |
| ١٢-وَبَنَيْنَا فَوْقَكُمْ | *Wa-banai-Nā fawqa-kum* | We have built above you |
| سَبْعًا شِدَاداً | *sab'an shidādā(n)* | seven strong (heavens) |
| ١٣-وَجَعَلْنَا | *Wa-ja'al-nā* | And We made |
| سِرَاجًا وَهَّاجًا | *sirājan wahhājā(n)* | a lamp blazing, dazzling |
| ١٤-وَأَنزَلْنَا | *Wa-'anzal-nā* | And We sent down |
| مِنَ ٱلْمُعْصِرَاتِ | *mina-(a)l-mu'ṣirāti* | from the rainy clouds |
| مَآءً ثَجَّاجًا | *mā'an thajjājā(n)* | water in abundance |
| ١٥-لِنُخْرِجَ بِهِ | *Li-nukhrija bi-hī* | That We produce, therewith |
| حَبًّا وَنَبَاتًا | *ḥabban wa-nabātā(n)* | grain and vegetable |
| ١٦-وَجَنَّٰتٍ أَلْفَافًا | *Wa-jannātin 'alfāfā(n)* | And gardens of luxurious foliage |
| ١٧- إِنَّ يَوْمَ ٱلْفَصْلِ | *'Inna Yawma-(a)l-Faṣli* | Indeed the Day of Decision, A Day of Sorting out |
| كَانَ مِيقَٰتًا | *kāna mīqātā(n)* | is a fixed time |
| ١٨-يَوْمَ يُنْفَخُ | *Yawma yunfakhu* | The Day will be blown, |
| فِي ٱلصُّورِ | *fī-(a)ṣ-Ṣūri* | in the Trumpet |
| فَتَأْتُونَ أَفْوَاجًا | *fa-ta'tūna 'afwājā(n)* | you will come forth in crowds |

| | | |
|---|---|---|
| ١٩-وَفُتِحَتِ ٱلسَّمَآءُ | *Wa-futiḥati-s-samā'u* | And will be open the heaven |
| فَكَانَتْ أَبْوَابًا | *fa-kānat 'abwābā(n)* | and becomes as gates |
| ٢٠-وَسُيِّرَتِ ٱلْجِبَالُ | *Wa-suyyirati-(a)l-jibālu* | And will set in motion the mountains |
| فَكَانَتْ سَرَابًا | *fa-kānat sarābā(n)* | as if they were a mirage |
| ٢١-إِنَّ جَهَنَّمَ | *'Inna jahannama* | Truly the Hell |
| كَانَتْ مِرْصَادًا | *kānat mirṣādā(n)* | is a place of ambush |
| ٢٢-لِّلطَّٰغِينَ | *Li-(a)ṭ-ṭāghīna* | For the rebellious, transgressors |
| مَآبًا | *ma'ābā(n)* | a destination, a home |
| ٢٣-لَّٰبِثِينَ فِيهَآ | *Lābithīna fī-hā* | Will abide in it, will live in it |
| أَحْقَابًا | *'aḥqābā(n)* | (for) ages |
| ٢٤-لَا يَذُوقُونَ | *La yadhūqūna* | will neither taste |
| فِيهَا بَرْدًا | *fī-hā bardan* | in it coolness |
| وَلَا شَرَابًا | *wa-lā sharābā(n)* | nor drink |
| ٢٥-إِلَّا حَمِيمًا | *'Illā ḥamīman* | Except boiling water |
| وَغَسَّاقًا | *wa-ghassāqā(n)* | and intensely cold |

*Lesson 24*

# *AN-NABA', 78:26-40*

## THE (GREAT) NEWS / THE TIDING

**Revealed in Makkah**

| **TRANSLITERATION:** | **ARABIC TEXT:** |
|---|---|
| 26. *Jazā'an wifāqa(n)* | -جَزَآءً وِّفَاقًا ○ |
| 27. *'Inna-hum kānū lā yarjūna ḥisābā(n)* | -إِنَّهُمْ كَانُوْا لَا يَرْجُوْنَ حِسَابًا ○ |
| 28. *Wa kadhdhabū bi-'āyātinā kidhdhābā(n)* | -وَكَذَّبُوْا بِاٰيٰتِنَا كِذَّابًا ○ |
| 29. *Wa kulla shai'in 'aḥṣainā-hu kitābā(n)* | -وَكُلَّ شَيْءٍ أَحْصَيْنٰهُ كِتٰبًا ○ |
| 30. *Fa-dhūqū fa-lan nazīda-kum'illā 'adhābā(n)* | -فَذُوْقُوْا فَلَنْ نَّزِيْدَكُمْ إِلَّا عَذَابًا ○ |
| 31. *'Inna li-(a)l-muttaqīna mafāzā(n)* | -إِنَّ لِلْمُتَّقِيْنَ مَفَازًا ○ |
| 32. *Ḥadā'iqa wa 'a'nābā(n)* | -حَدَآئِقَ وَأَعْنَابًا ○ |
| 33. *Wa kawā'iba 'atrābā(n)* | -وَّكَوَاعِبَ أَتْرَابًا ○ |
| 34. *Wa ka'san dihāqā(n)* | -وَّكَأْسًا دِهَاقًا ○ |
| 35. *Lā yasma'ūna fī-hā laghwan wa lā kidhdhābā(n)* | -لَا يَسْمَعُوْنَ فِيْهَا لَغْوًا وَّلَا كِذّٰبًا ○ |
| 36. *Jazā'an min Rabbi-ka 'aṭā'an ḥisābā(n)* | -جَزَآءً مِّنْ رَّبِّكَ عَطَآءً حِسَابًا ○ |
| 37. *Rabbi-(a)s-samāwāti wa-(a)l-'arḍi wa mā baina-huma-* | -رَّبِّ السَّمٰوٰتِ وَالْأَرْضِ وَمَا بَيْنَهُمَا |
| *(a)r-Raḥmāni lā-yamlikūna min-hu khiṭābā(n)* | الرَّحْمٰنِ لَا يَمْلِكُوْنَ مِنْهُ خِطَابًا ○ |
| 38. *Yawma yaqūmu-(a)r-Rūḥu wa-(a)l-malā'ikatu ṣaffan* | -يَوْمَ يَقُوْمُ الرُّوْحُ وَالْمَلٰٓئِكَةُ صَفًّا |
| *lā-yatakallamūna 'illā man 'adhina* | لَا يَتَكَلَّمُوْنَ إِلَّا مَنْ أَذِنَ |
| *la-hu-(a)r-Raḥmānu wa qāla ṣawābā(n)* | لَهُ الرَّحْمٰنُ وَقَالَ صَوَابًا ○ |

39. *__Dh__ālika-(a)l-yawmu-(a)l-ḥaqq-u fa-man*

*__sh__ā'a-(a)t-ta__kh__a__dh__a 'ilā Rabbi-hī ma'ābā(n)*

40. *'Innā 'an__dh__arnā-kum 'a__dh__āban qarīban*

*yawma yanẓuru-(a)l-mar'u mā qaddamat*

*yadā-hu wa-yaqūlu-(a)l-kāfiru*

*yālaitanī kuntu turābā(n)*

-ذٰلِكَ الْيَوْمُ الْحَقُّ ۚ فَمَنْ
شَآءَ اتَّخَذَ إِلٰى رَبِّهٖ مَاٰبًا ○
-إِنَّآ أَنْذَرْنٰكُمْ عَذَابًا قَرِيْبًا ۚ
يَّوْمَ يَنْظُرُ الْمَرْءُ مَا قَدَّمَتْ
يَدٰهُ وَيَقُوْلُ الْكٰفِرُ
يٰلَيْتَنِيْ كُنْتُ تُرٰبًا ○

**__TRANSLATIONS__:**

26. A fitting recompense (for them).
27. For that they used not to fear any account (for their deeds)
28. But they (impudently) treated Our Signs as false.
29. And all things have We preserved on record.
30. "So taste you (the fruits of your deeds) for not increase shall We grant you, except in punishment."
31. Truly for the Righteous there will be a fulfillment of (the Heart's) desires;
32. Gardens enclosed, and grapevines;
33. Companions of Equal Age;
34. And Cup full (to the Brim)
35. No Vanity shall they hear in it, nor untruth;
36. Recompense from your Lord, a gift (amply) sufficient,
37. (From) the Lord of the heavens and the earth and all between, (Allāh) Most-Gracious; none shall have power to argue with Him.

26. Reward proportioned (to their evil deeds)
27. For lo! they looked not for a reckoning;
28. They called Our revelations false with strong denial.
29. Everything have We recorded in a Book.
30. So taste (of that which you have earned). No increase do We give you save of torment.
31. Lo! for the duteous is achievement-
32. Gardens enclosed and vineyards,
33. And maidens for companions,
34. And a full cup.
35. There hear they never vain discourse, nor lying-
36. Requital from your Lord- a gift in payment-
37. Lord of the heavens and the earth, and (all) that is between them, the Beneficent with whom none can converse.

38. The day that the Spirit and the angels will stand forth in ranks, none shall speak except any who is permitted by (Allāh) most gracious and he will say what is right.
39. The Day will be the sure Reality: therefore, whoso will, let him take a (straight) return to his Lord!
40. Truly, We have warned you of a Penalty near, the Day when man will see (the Deeds) which his hands have sent forth, and the Unbeliever will say, "woe to me! would that I were (mere) dust"

38. On the day when the angels and the Spirit stand arrayed, they speak not, saving him whom the Beneficent allows and who speaks right.
39. That is the True Day. So whoso will, should seek recourse to his Lord.
40. Lo! We warn you of a doom at hand, a day whereon a man will look on that which his own hands have sent forth before, and the disbelievers will cry: "Would that I were dust!"

---

**EXPLANATION**:

78:26-30. This will be their reward for whatever evil they did on this Earth (v. 25-26). While alive, they disbelieved in Judgment Day and denied the Signs of Allāh سبحانه وتعالى ; and they will see that all of their actions had been recorded by Allāh سبحانه وتعالى. On this Day, they will receive their due punishment (v. 27-30).

78:31-37. The righteous man, who attended to his duties for Allāh سبحانه وتعالى, will receive all that his heart desires (v. 31).

The description of human desires is reported at a level that human beings may understand and appreciate. However, all the pleasures of *Jannah* are incomparable to what we regard as pleasurable things in our life experience on Earth. These must be understood on both the spiritual and practical levels.

The rewards of *Jannah* include enclosed gardens, young companions and cups full to the brim with any desired drinks (v. 32-34).

Rasūlullāh ﷺ informed us that the believers will enter *Jannah* in the best physical form. Life after Resurrection will be of the highest perfection, both physical and spiritual, for the believer.

In addition, *Jannah* will be a place of innocence, purity and spirituality. There will be no talk of vanity, falsehood or deception (v. 35).

These pleasures, and others, will be a most generous gift of Allāh's سبحانه وتعالى Mercy as reward for the good deeds of the believers (v. 36). Allāh سبحانه وتعالى is the Owner and Lord of the Heavens, the Earth and whatever lies between them; no one will have power on that Day to argue with Him about His rewards or punishments (v. 37).

78:38-39. The Day of Judgment will be a very special Day. As people gather for Judgment, the Angels, led by the *Rūḥ,* Angel Jibrīl عليه السلام will form lines beside the Throne of the Lord. All will be in awe, respectfully quiet, no one will speak, except with the permission of Allāh سبحانه وتعالى in His infinite Mercy. On that Day, every hidden thing will be revealed, thus no one will be able to hide or tell a lie. Everyone will speak the truth (v. 38).

The reality and the truth of that Day is well confirmed, thus let anyone desiring the pleasure of Allāh سبحانه وتعالى take the path of Righteousness while there is still time (v. 39).

78:40. Allāh سبحانه وتعالى warns us that the coming of the Day is a true and certain event. On that Day, each individual will see the actions that he had sent forth. On that Day, all actions, intentions and feelings will be accounted for and evaluated. On that Day, the unbeliever will wish to be dust, without life. Therefore, the time is now to repent and to turn to Allāh سبحانه وتعالى and to commit to spending one's life in accordance with His Command.

**WE HAVE LEARNED:**

* The Day of Judgment is a certainty but no one knows the exact time when it would come.
* The Righteous will be given their best form to enjoy the pleasure of the *Jannah.*
* The wicked, confronting punishment, would like to become dust and ashes.

## VOCABULARY

٧٨- سُورَةُ ٱلنَّبَإِ

| | | |
|---|---|---|
| ٢٦-جَزَآءً وِفَاقًا | *Jazā'an wifāqā(n)* | A reward fitting |
| ٢٧-إِنَّهُمْ | *'Inna-hum* | Indeed they |
| كَانُوا لَا يَرْجُونَ | *kānū la yarjūna* | used not to hope |
| حِسَابًا | *ḥisābā(n)* | for any account |
| ٢٨-وَكَذَّبُوا | *Wa-kadhdhabū* | And they denied |
| بِآيَـٰتِنَا | *bi-'āyāti-Nā* | (to) Our Revelations, (to) Our Signs |
| كِذَّابًا | *kidhdhābā* | a strong denial |
| ٢٩-وَكُلَّ شَيْءٍ | *Wa-kulla shai'in* | And every thing |
| أَحْصَيْنَٰهُ كِتَـٰبًا | *'aḥsai-nā-hu kitābā(n)* | We have recorded it in a book |

| | | |
|---|---|---|
| ٣٠-فَذُوقُوا | *Fa-dhūqū* | So taste |
| فَلَنْ نَّزِيْدَكُمْ | *fa-lan nazīda-kum* | We shall not increase you |
| إِلاَّ عَذَابًا | *'illa 'adhābā(n)* | except in punishment |
| ٣١-إِنَّ لِلْمُتَّقِيْنَ | *'Inna li-(a)l-muttaqīna* | Verily for the righteous |
| مَفَازًا | *mafāzā(n)* | is an achievement |
| ٣٢-حَدَآئِقَ وَأَعْنَـٰبًا | *Ḥadā'iqa wa-'a'nābā(n)* | Enclosed gardens and grapevines |
| ٣٣-وَكَوَاعِبَ أَتْرَابًا | *Wa-kawā'iba 'atrābā(n)* | And maidens (of equal age) for companions |
| ٣٤-وَكَأْسًا دِهَاقًا | *Wa-ka'san dihāqā(n)* | A cup full |
| ٣٥-لا يَسْمَعُونَ | *La yasma'ūna* | They do not hear |
| فِيهَا لَغوًا | *fī-hā laghwan* | in it, vain talk |
| وَلاَ كِذَّابًا | *wa-la kidhdhābā(n)* | nor lying |
| ٣٦-جَزَآءً مِّن رَّبِّكَ | *Jazā'an min Rabbi-ka* | A reward from your Lord |
| عَطَآءً حِسَابًا | *'aṭā'an ḥisābā(n)* | a gift sufficient (in) payment |
| ٣٧-ربِّ ٱلسَّمَـٰوَاتِ | *Rabbi-(a)s-samāwāti* | The Lord of Heavens |
| وَٱلأَرْضِ | *wa-(a)l-'arḍi* | and the Earth |
| وَمَا بَيْنَهُمَا | *wa-mā baina-humā* | and whatever is in between |
| ٱلرَّحْمَـٰنِ | *'Ar-Raḥmān(i)* | the Most Gracious, the Beneficent |
| لا يَمْلِكُونَ | *la yamlikūna* | none has power |
| مِنْهُ خِطَابًا | *min-Hu khiṭābā(n)* | to argue with Him |
| ٣٨- يَومَ | *Yawma* | The day |
| يَقُومُ ٱلرُّوحُ | *yaqūmu-(a)r-Rūḥu* | will stand the Spirit |

| | | |
|---|---|---|
| وَٱلْمَلَٰٓئِكَةُ | *wa-(a)l-malā'ikatu* | and the angels |
| صَفّاً | *ṣaffan* | in ranks |
| لَا يَتَكَلَّمُونَ | *la yatakallamūna* | they do not speak |
| إِلَّا مَنْ | *'illā man* | Except the one |
| أَذِنَ لَهُ | *'a<u>dh</u>ina la-hū* | who is permitted |
| ٱلرَّحْمَٰنُ | *'Ar-Raḥmān(u)* | by the Most-Gracious |
| وَقَالَ صَوَابًا | *wa-qāla ṣawābā(n)* | and he say what is right |
| ٣٩-ذَٰلِكَ ٱلْيَوْمُ | *<u>Dh</u>ālika-(a)l-Yawmu* | That Day (is) |
| ٱلْحَقُّ | *'al-Ḥaqqu* | the True |
| فَمَنْ شَآءَ | *fa-man <u>sh</u>ā'a* | who so will |
| ٱتَّخَذَ | *'itta<u>kh</u>a<u>dh</u>a* | let him take |
| إِلَىٰ رَبِّهِۦ | *'ilā Rabbi-hī* | to his Lord |
| مَـَٔابًا | *ma'ābā(n)* | recourse, return, protection |
| ٤٠-إِنَّا أَنذَرْنَٰكُمْ | *'Inna 'an<u>dh</u>ar-nā-kum* | Verily, We warn you |
| عَذَابًا قَرِيبًا | *'a<u>dh</u>āban qarīban* | of chastisement near, punishment close by |
| يَوْمَ يَنظُرُ ٱلْمَرْءُ | *yawma yanẓuru-(a)l-mar'u* | the day when man (a human) will see |
| مَا قَدَّمَتْ يَدَاهُ | *mā qaddamat yadā-hu* | whatever his hands sent forth |
| وَيَقُولُ ٱلْكَافِرُ | *wa-yaqūlu-(a)l-kāfiru* | and the *kāfir* (will) say |
| يَٰلَيْتَنِى | *yā-laitanī* | woe unto me! |
| كُنتُ تُرَٰبًا | *kuntu turābā(n)* | would that I were dust |

## Appendix I

# THE SIGN OF THE 'ĀYAH

Every language has its signs of writing, the punctuation marks, to guide the reader through various parts of the speech. Without punctuation marks it is often difficult to make exact sense. In English we use the signs of ,.;:'"? to help proper reading.

Punctuation marks are more important in Arabic; it is the language of the Revelation and must be read and understood exactly as it was revealed, recited and understood by Rasūlullāh ﷺ and his *Ṣaḥābah* ﵃. Arabic writing was in its initial stage when the Qur'ān was revealed. Muslims not only developed an elaborate system of writing to preserve the exact pronunciation of Arabic text, they also preserved systems of reading for preserving the ways in which the Qur'ān was recited by Rasūlullāh ﷺ and his *Ṣaḥābah.*

The Qur'ānic Arabic *'Āyah,* a circular sign (o), is used to indicate various types of pauses or stops. There are further letter signs placed on the *'Āyah* to indicate what kind of stop that is. There are also other signs in the Qur'ān to help read each verse properly. The best way to learn the Qur'ān is through a teacher; a well prepared text and audio and videos could also help a great deal. All *'Āyah* signs and other signs must be learned properly and followed carefully in reading the Qur'ān. To facilitate reading the *Transliteration* in the *Juz'* we have used end of the *'Āyāt* as *al-waqf al-muṭlaq* (absolute stop), even when we had the option to continue. In Arabic regular ending of the last word often changes before *'Āyah.* Some *ḥarakāt* are replaced and some letters are interchanged. In this **textbook** we have placed the silent *ḥarakah* or *ḥarakāt* inside brackets and new letter which replaces *ḥarakāt* (in case it happens) is added before the bracket, in **bold.** Once a reader learns the proper recitation he / she can go with the options.

Here are the signs:

O : sign of an *'Āyah* ( آيَة ), follow the sign on it; if no sign then stop.

ط : *Al-Waqf al-Muṭlaq* ( اَلْوَقْفُ الْمُطلَق ), Absolute Stop; stop is compulsory, the subject continues.

م : *Al-Waqf al-Lāzim* ( اَلْوَقْفُ اللاَّزِم ), Compulsory Stop; no stopping changes the meaning.

ج : *Al-Waqf al-Jā'iz* ( اَلْوَقْفُ الْجَائِز ), Permissible Stop; better to stop, to continue is allowed.

لا : *Lā* ( لاَ ), No; stop is optional, does not affect the meaning.

ز : *Al-Waqf al-Mujawwaz*( اَلوقفُ اَلمجَوَّز ), Permitted Stop; permitted to stop, better to continue.

صۡ : *Al-Waqf al-Murakhkhaṣ*, ( ٱلۡوَقۡفُ ٱلۡمُرَخَّصُ ), preferable to continue; stopping is permitted.

صلے : *Al-Waṣl al-'Awlā*, ( ٱلۡوَصۡلُ الأَوۡلَىٰ ), Preferred Connection; preferable to continue.

ق : *Qīla 'alaihi al-Waqf* ( قِيلَ عَلَيۡهِ ٱلۡوَقۡفُ ), Stop Obligatory; must stop.

صل : *Qad Yūṣal* ( قَدۡ يُوصَلُ ), both stop or continuation permitted.

قف : *Qif* ( قِفۡ ), Stop; a complete stop ordered.

لا : *Lā* ( لاَ ), No; no stop when inside the text.

ك : *Kadhālika*, ( كَذَٰلِكَ ), Same as Before; previous sign must be followed.

وقفة : *Waqfah* ( وَقۡفَةٌ ), Long Breath; take a long breath then continue without stopping.

س سكتة : *Saktah* ( سَكۡتَةٌ ), Short Breath; take a small breath then continue without break.

**Appendix II**

# IQRA'
# TRANSLITERATION CHART

| | | | | | | | | |
|---|---|---|---|---|---|---|---|---|
| q | ق | * | z | ز | | ' | أء | * |
| k | ك | | s | س | | b | ب | |
| l | ل | | sh | ش | | t | ت | |
| m | م | | s | ص | * | th | ث | * |
| n | ن | | d | ض | * | j | ج | |
| h | هـ | | t | ط | * | h | ح | * |
| w | و | | z | ظ | * | kh | خ | * |
| y | ي | | ، | ع | * | d | د | |
| | | | gh | غ | * | dh | ذ | * |
| | | | f | ف | | r | ر | |

| SHORT VOWELS | LONG VOWELS | DIPHTHONGS |
|---|---|---|
| a ـَـ | ā ـَا | aw ـَوْ |
| u ـُـ | ū ـُو | ai ـَيْ |
| i ـِـ | ī ـِي | |
| Such as: *kataba* كَتَبَ | Such as: *Kitāb* كِتَاب | Such as: *Lawḥ* لَوْح |
| Such as: *Qul* قُلْ | Such as: *Mamnūn* مَمْنُون | Such as: *'Ain* عَيْن |
| Such as: *Ni'mah* نِعْمَة | Such as: *Dīn* دِين | |

* Special attention should be given to the symbols marked with stars for they have no equivalent in the English sounds .

**** Special Note on the Transliteration of Words Involving the Definite Article al* (ال)**

- There are situations where the alif ( ا ) of the Definite Article is not pronounced though it is present in writing. To account for this type of 'Alif in the transliteration system, we have added an (a) in parenthesis before the Lam.

Example :
Al-Ḥamdu li Allāhi Rabbi al-'Ālamīn, is written as
Al-Ḥamdu li-(A)llāhi Rabbi (a)l-Ālamīn ,and read as
Al-Ḥamdu li-llāhi Rabbi-l-'Ālamīn

# ISLAMIC INVOCATIONS:

Rasūlullāh, *Ṣalla Allahu 'alaihi wa Sallam* (صَلَّى ٱللَّهُ عَلَيْهِ وَسَلَّمَ), and the Qur'ān teach us to glorify Allah (SWT) when we mention His Name and to invoke His Blessings when we mention the names of His Angels, Messengers, the *Ṣaḥābah* and the Pious Ancestors.

When we mention the Name of Allah we must say: *Subḥāna-hu Wa-Ta'ālā* (سُبْحَانَهُ وَتَعَالَى), Glorified is He and High. In this book we write (SWT) to remind us to Glorify Allah.

When we mention the name of Rasūlullāh (S) we must say: *Ṣalla Allāhu 'alai-hi wa-Sallam,* (صَلَّى ٱللَّهُ عَلَيْهِ وَسَلَّمَ), May Allah's Blessings and Peace be upon him.
We write an (Ṣ) to remind us to invoke Allah's Blessings on Rasūlullāh.

When we mention the name of an angel or a prophet we must say: *Alai-hi-s-Salām* (عَلَيْهِ ٱلسَّلَامُ), Upon him be peace.
We write an (A) to remind us to invoke Allah's Peace upon him.

When we hear the name of the *Ṣaḥābah* we must say:
For more than two, *Raḍiy-Allahu Ta'ālā 'anhum,* (رَضِيَ ٱللَّهُ تَعَالَى عَنْهُمْ), May Allah be pleased with them.
For two of them, *Raḍiy-Allahu Ta'ālā 'an-humā* (رَضِيَ ٱللَّهُ تَعَالَى عَنْهُمَا), May Allah be pleased with both of them.
For a *Ṣaḥābī, Raḍiy-Allahu Ta'ālā 'an-hu* (رَضِيَ ٱللَّهُ تَعَالَى عَنْهُ), May Allah be pleased with him.
For a *Ṣaḥābiyyah, Raḍiy-Allahu Ta'ālā 'an-hā* (رَضِيَ ٱللَّهُ تَعَالَى عَنْهَا), May Allah be pleased with her.
We write (R) to remind us to invoke Allah's Pleasure with a *Ṣaḥābī* or with *Ṣaḥābah.*

When we hear the name of the Pious Ancestor *(As-Salaf as-Ṣāliḥ)* we must say.
For a man, *Raḥmatullāh 'alaihi* (رَحْمَةُ ٱللَّهِ عَلَيْهِ), May Allah's Mercy be upon him.
For a woman, *Raḥmatullāh 'alai-hā* (رَحْمَةُ ٱللَّهِ عَلَيْهَا), May Allah's Mercy be with her.

APPENDIX IV:

# GLOSSARY

| | |
|---|---|
| **Abode** | Home |
| **Adhere** | Attach, fasten, stick |
| **Admonish** | To warn, to caution, to rebuke in a gentle manner |
| **Adversity** | Problem, misfortune |
| ***Al-'Ākhirah*** | Day of Judgment, Hereafter |
| **Astray** | Going away from the right path |
| **Authentic** | Reliable |
| **Calamity** | Great misfortune |
| **Catastrophic** | A disastrous end, great misfortune |
| **Commotion** | A great disturbance, social or political upheaval |
| **Comprehend** | Understand, grasp, discern |
| **Conform** | To adapt, adjust or agree |
| **Confrontation** | Dispute, clash |
| **Controversy** | Argument, dispute |
| **Convulsion** | Great disturbance, a violent change |
| **Cosmic** | Universal, vast, extra-terrestrial |
| **Cosmology** | Study of the origin of the Universe and its structure |
| ***Dā'ī*** | A preacher, one who gives *Da'wah* |
| **Day of Chastisement** | Day of Judgment, *Al-'Ākhirah* |
| **Defiance** | Open opposition, bold resistance, a challenge |
| **Downcast** | Depressed, humiliated |
| **Emphatically** | Forcefully, with emphasis in speech |
| **Exertion** | Strong pressure, struggle |
| **Exile** | To expel from one's native country, to banish |
| ***Fir'awn*** | Pharaoh; title used by the Ancient Egyptian Kings |
| **Glorify** | High praise |
| **Goblet** | A drinking glass |
| **Horizon** | Boundary between earth and sky |
| **Hostile** | Not friendly, showing enmity |
| **Humiliate** | To make someone feel ashamed |
| **Impermanence** | Temporary, not permanent |
| **Impurity** | Contamination, adulteration, foulness |
| **Infinite** | Endless in time and space |
| **Inheritance** | Anything passing from one to the successors, heritage |
| **Integrity** | Honesty, decency |
| **Interpretation** | Explanation |

| | |
|---|---|
| *Jahannam* | Hell |
| *Jannah* | Paradise |
| *Lawḥ Maḥfūẓ* | Preserved Tablets, Tablets on which Qur'ān is guarded |
| **Miracle** | Any happening by Divine power which is beyond normal, a wonder |
| **Mock** | To make fun by imitating someone's action or speech |
| **Murky** | Very dark, not clear |
| **Oath** | A pledge, vow, to call God or something important as a witness |
| **Obstinacy** | to be stubborn |
| **Oppress** | To crush by force, to suppress |
| **Ornate** | Fancy, showy, flamboyant |
| **Overwhelming** | Completely overpowering, very powerful |
| **Persecuting** | Victimizing, torturing or abusing |
| **Phenomenon** | Event, happening |
| **Potential** | Possible, dormant |
| **Prevalent** | Current, popular |
| **Proportional** | In accordance with |
| **Prostrate** | To cast (oneself) face down on the ground in submission |
| **Recompose** | To rearrange, to rewrite |
| **Reprisal** | Retaliation, vengeance |
| **Resurrection** | Act of rising again, rising from the dead |
| **Revelation** | *Waḥī,* Allāh's disclosure of Himself or His Will to someone |
| **Righteousness** | Quality of being morally right, *the Taqwā* |
| **Shrub** | A small plant that grows throughout the year |
| **Squander** | To spend wastefully |
| **Strained** | Forced, stressed |
| **Stubble** | Stalks left on the ground after the crop is cut |
| **Supplicate** | To beg, plead or pray humbly |
| **Sustain** | To support or feed |
| *Suwar* | (Plural of *Sūrāh*), Chapters (of Qur'ān) |
| **Testimony** | Proof, a statement of facts, evidence |
| **Transgress** | To violate, disobey or trespass |
| **Transient** | A temporary or passing (stage) |
| **Tribulation** | Trial, hardship, affliction |
| **Triumph** | Victory, success |
| **Unnerving** | To make nervous |

*IQRA' International Educational Foundation* (Chicago, IL), a non-profit Islamic Educational trust, was established in 1983 by concerned Muslims in response to the growing need of systematic Islamic education for our children and youth.

**We invite you to help IQRA' develop into a major center for research and production of Islamic educational materials by:**

i. *Becoming Ansars of IQRA' Educational Program; contributing regularly to its pioneering efforts.*

ii. *Joining the IQRA' Book Club, making a commitment to buy one IQRA' book each month as it is published.*

## *IQRA' QUR'AN PROJECT:*

IQRA' is considering to serialize the publication of the entire Qur'an on this pattern in sixty bi-monthly installments (that is half a Juz' every two months, each installment needing a subscription (tax-deductible) of $100 a year or more. Each subscriber will receive the publications free. We need an intitial committment of 5000 people before launching the project.

We will greatly appreciate your prompt response for participation. We do not want any contributions for this project at the moment. However, interested participants and sponsers are requested to contact us to indicate their interest.

**Abidullah Ghazi,** M. A. Political Science (Alig), M. Sc. Econ. (LSE, London), Ph. D. Comparative Religions (Harvard)

Dr. Abidullah Ghazi, Executive Director of IQRA' International Educational Foundation, and his wife, Dr. Tasneema Ghazi, Director of Curriculum, are co-founders of IQRA' International Educational Foundation (a non-profit Islamic educational trust) and Chief Editors of its Educational Program. They have combined their talents and expertise and dedicated their lives to produce a Comprehensive Program of Islamic Studies for our children and youth and to develop IQRA' into a major center of research and development for Islamic Studies, specializing in Islamic education.

Dr. Abidullah Ghazi, a specialist in Islamic Studies and Comparative Religion, belongs to a prominent family of the Ulama' of India. His family has been active in the field of Islamic education, *da'wah*, and struggle for freedom. Dr. Ghazi's early education was carried in traditional *Madaris*. He has studied at Muslim University, Aligarh, The London School of Economics, and Harvard University. He has taught at the Universities of Jamia Millia Islamia, Delhi, London, Harvard, San Diego, Minnesota, Northwestern, Governors State and King Abdul Aziz University, Jeddah. He is a consultant for the development of the program of Islamic Studies in various schools and universities. He is a well–known community worker, speaker, writer and poet.